# 11 Reasons Families Succeed

## RICHARD & RITA TATE

# 11 Reasons
# Families
# Succeed

## ABOUT PHOTOCOPYING THIS BOOK

First Timothy 5:17-18 instructs us to give the laborer his wages, specifically those who labor in the Word and doctrine. Hensley Publishing has a moral, as well as legal, responsibility to see that out authors receive fair compensation for their efforts. Many of them depend upon the income for the sale of their books as their sole livelihood. So, for that matter, do the artists, printers, and numerous other people who work to make these books available to you. Please help us by discouraging those who would copy this material in lieu of purchase.

HENSLEY
PUBLISHING

ISBN 1-56322-081-4

# 11 Reasons Families Succeed

# ENDORSEMENTS

*For years I have encouraged my friends, Richard and Rita Tate, to take the information they have learned working with families across America and write a book. Finally, 11 Reasons Families Succeed is available to us all. It should be required reading for every couple planning to marry. Every counselor and pastor in America should have a copy too!*
—MARK VICTOR HANSEN, AUTHOR
  CHICKEN SOUP FOR THE SOUL

*Richard and Rita Tate have made it simple. Do the things they teach in their wonderful book, 11 Reasons Families Succeed, and you will find your family begin to succeed. They examine the needs of men and women as well as the basic needs of every child. These are eternal issues made as fresh and new as the morning paper. We are delighted that the Tates are a vital part of the statewide marriage initiative in Oklahoma. We believe their book will become a gold standard for marriages and single-parent families across our nation.*
—THE HONORABLE FRANK AND CATHY KEATING
  GOVERNOR AND FIRST LADY OF OKLAHOMA

*Richard and Rita Tate capture the essence of God's plan for the family when they express in 11 Reasons Families Succeed, "God does not want your family to simply work, He wants it to SUCCEED!" The first time I was privileged to hear them teach, I knew I wanted my family to practice the principles they shared. As a wife and mother I thank the Tates for this wonderful, helpful book.*
—KELLYE CASH SHEPHERD
  MISS AMERICA 1989

*Every child deserves to have the physical nourishment they need, and every family should have the spiritual nourishment 11 Reasons Families Succeed provides. Richard and Rita Tate have taken the principles of the Word of God and coupled them with their experiences to give us a tool which is understandable, easy to apply and immensely powerful. We have known the Tates and their family for almost thirty years and are pleased that what we have seen lived out is now in print!*
—LARRY AND FRANCES JONES
  FOUNDERS, FEED THE CHILDREN

# TABLE OF CONTENTS

# ACKNOWLEDGEMENTS

*Thine, O L*ORD *is the greatness...and the glory...and thou art exalted as head above all.*
—*I Chronicles 29:11*

*I will not give my glory unto another...I am the first, and I also am the last.*
—*Isaiah 48:11-12*

The above verses clearly express that all praise and glory belongs to God. We should never touch His glory or pass it to any individual. However, Proverb 3:27 tells us God insists we express our thanks to those who have helped us along the way.

*Withhold not good from them to whom it is due, when it is in the power of thine hand to do it.*

With that verse as our guide, we offer our deepest thanks to five individuals. Without them this book would never have become the reality it is today. To God be the eternal glory, but to each of them we offer our eternal thanks!

## MARK VICTOR HANSEN

AMERICA'S MASTER MOTIVATOR AND AUTHOR OF *CHICKEN SOUP FOR THE SOUL*
*You will never know how much your wisdom, insight, and belief in us over the years has meant. How could we ever forget your encouragement to "ink it, don't think it!" The ink may finally be dry, but our thanks for your friendship will be a continuing journal.*

## DR. GENE AND DOROTHY HELLSTERN

*God has used you in our lives over and over again, and this book is one more example of His place for you in our family and marriage. It would never have become a reality without your encouraging words, faith in us, and being there for us at the right time.*

**NEAL HENSLEY**

PRESIDENT, HENSLEY PUBLISHING

*We are proud and honored to be a part of Hensley Publishing's family and cannot thank you enough for your belief in this project and the goal of your company to help families across America and around the world to not just "work" but to succeed!*

**TERRI KALFAS**

DIRECTOR OF PUBLISHING, HENSLEY PUBLISHING

*You are the consummate professional. Thank you for believing in this book and in us. Your help in bringing our ideas to life and formulating concepts was invaluable.*

# FOREWORD

When we realized our parents were going to write a book about the family, not one of us was surprised. As a matter of fact, many years ago David said it would happen. We asked if we could write this foreword and share with you, the reader, a few of our thoughts about the journey Mom and Dad describe.

The experiences you have had, and may be having now in your family, will probably not mirror the experiences we had in ours. Regardless of where you are your family has not only the opportunity but also the responsibility to work together toward the goal of a strong, successful family.

We didn't wake up one morning and realize our family had all the answers. Our parents taught us that the great joy in life is to seek the truth. Having parents who determined to have the Lord and His truth at the center of our family has literally saved us. There were times we were brought to our knees by the cruel realities of life. We survived these times, not as individuals, but as a family!

When times are hard, we tend to question the things in which we believe the most. You may have trouble believing in your family from time to time as challenges come. Don't give up! Take pride in your family. Take ownership of the task of making your family as strong as it can be for the entire world to see. Look into your wife's eyes and say "thank you." Hug your sons for no reason at all. Smile when your daughter enters the room. Play house, have tea parties, make cookies, laugh out loud, and wrestle in the middle of the living room floor.

We learned that the first step to joy in a family is for each person to create joy within themselves, even when there may be nothing to be joyful about.

Our family is not perfect by any means, but we never stopped believing in one another. Our parents were far from perfect (we knew that firsthand!), but they always sought to do the right thing.

We are all adults now. Grandchildren have come along, and we have become the family we are because two people decided to rear us in a Christ-centered, love-filled environment. Richard and Rita Tate never settled for anything less. They never gave up on us even when everything seemed in disarray. They showed us the power of prayer and made spending time with us their priority. After we left to create our own lives and families, they found themselves with an "empty nest." It was at that time they felt led to share with the world all they have learned about parenting.

This book is a huge blessing to our family because it reveals where we have been and how we have fought to be where we are today. We still have our differences and downfalls, but we now see the value of dealing with them with love and respect.

Open your heart and mind to the principles in this book and let God speak to you. We were the "testing ground" for each one. We know that as you read this book you will be blessed by the teachings of Richard and Rita Tate. We, the products of every page, invite you to be as blessed by our parents as we have been throughout our lives!

Thanks Mom and Dad. We are so proud of you!

# INTRODUCTION

*An ounce of prevention is worth a pound of cure.*
*—Benjamin Franklin*

## "DIVORCE BELT"

The three-inch-high letters of the *Tulsa World's* headline glared at us from the airport newspaper rack, stopping us dead in our tracks. It was the size of a headline usually reserved to announce the end of a world war or an astronaut landing on the moon. Sadly, this lead story was referring to our home state of Oklahoma.

How could Oklahoma, the buckle of the "Bible belt," have become the "divorce belt?" This was not a great honor about which we could be proud. It was impossible to believe that in a state where there is one church for every 112 people, the greatest number of divorces were occurring in Christian marriages. What was going on? How could these marriages be failing at such an alarming rate?

We were to soon learn that the entire nation, not just the state of Oklahoma, was reeling under the effects of crumbling marriages and failing families. According to recent statistics, the per capita divorce rate in the USA is the highest of any country in the world. It appears that Generation "X" is rapidly becoming Generation "EX!"

*The only thing necessary for the triumph of evil is for good men to do nothing.*
*—EDMUND BURKE*

We knew we had to stop complaining about the problem and take some action. This book is our attempt to light the candle of God's truth, which can illuminate the way to solutions for this out-of-control problem. You will find answers in this book. You will find solutions and suggestions which are practical, biblical, easy to understand, useful, and immediately applicable.

*It is better to light one candle than curse the darkness.*
*—THE CHRISTOPHER SOCIETY*

Almost everyone with whom we speak about the issue agrees that there is a problem with dysfunctional families and the increasing divorce rate in America. The fact that you are reading this book indicates there is hope. You may be reading to seek help to overcome current problems or to strengthen your family and marriage. James 1:5 tells us *if any of you lack wisdom let him ask of God, that giveth to all men liberally and upbraideth not; and it shall be given unto him.* Perhaps you are seeking to find direction and answers in one of the darkest moments of your life. Possibly your marriage has already failed and you are faced with difficult decisions and complex issues regarding a former spouse or your children. Whatever the situation may be which has brought you to this point, congratulations. You are doing something positive about it and you are to be commended. We are praying that the Holy Spirit will do a great work as you open your heart to His leadership and admonitions.

*Do not turn back when you know the goal.*

—PUBLIUS SYRUS

We are sometimes asked to present our seminar, *11 Reasons Families Succeed,* "without making it a biblical thing." We reject each of those requests and make it clear to the person inviting us that without the basic principles of the Word of God there can be no truly successful marriages or families. Families might "survive," but without God at their center, they cannot genuinely succeed.

> *Keep the words of this covenant and do them, that you may be successful in all you do.*
> *—Deuteronomy 29:9*

We didn't set out to write a book about marriage and family issues. A few years after finishing college we noticed many of our friends were already in their second, third, and for some, fourth marriages. It became a "wake-up" call for us. The material in this book is the result of our personal determination to build a successful marriage. We didn't want to end up in divorce court and become another statistic.

To keep divorce from claiming our marriage and family, several times each year over the last twenty-five years of our marriage we've taken a weekend getaway to focus on the challenges of our marriage, our children, and our future. We play some golf and tennis and have a wonderful time, but the primary goal of these intimate two-person retreats has always been to develop a biblically based "marriage operations manual" by which we could live. We discovered an important principle many years ago at one of our retreats. If you will talk about an issue when it's not yet an issue, then hopefully it won't become an issue.

That principle became the basic philosophy of each retreat. It is extremely difficult to deal with marriage and family issues when emotions are running high. Don't wait until the dam breaks to try to make repairs. This study will help you deal with issues before they become destructive. The best defense is always a good offense. With this book you can take the offensive and attack the problems before they become insurmountable.

Sometimes we referred to our retreats as "divorce retreats." Why did we call them this? Because our goal was to be able to return home and report to our children that our *"divorce"* was in terrible shape; we loved each other, were committed to each other, and divorce would never be an option for their mom and dad!

A common fear that children have is the fear of being separated from their parents. It gave our children great comfort to know that their Mom and Dad were working on their marriage and were able to assure them their parents were not headed toward a divorce. Most of their friends had experienced divorce, so our words gave them great security. No divorce. Not now, not ever. They could sleep better at night, and so could we.

You might take this book and get away with your spouse for a few weekends to try a "divorce retreat" yourselves. It protected our marriage and consequently our family many times.

> *Jesus Christ the same yesterday, and today, and for ever. Be not carried about with divers and strange doctrines. For it is a good thing that the heart be established with grace.*
> —Hebrews 13:8-9

Each person, family, and marriage will respond to the principles in this book in a different way. Use the method that works best for you but always remember the following.

## METHODS ARE MANY; PRINCIPLES ARE FEW.

The principles found in the following eleven chapters come from notes compiled through the decades of our "divorce retreats," personal battles, victories, and failures. They have worked for us. They will work for you.

No marriage or family can reach its potential without a thorough saturation in the principles of God's Word. None of the principles in this book have their foundation in the wisdom of man or in the insights of Richard and Rita Tate. If you've tried to reason, analyze, rationalize, or "work out" your family and marriage problems on yout own, it is time to step away from your system and

It is essential to realize that whether you are a single parent, married, divorced, rearing your grandchildren, unmarried, a caregiver, or engaged to be married, you are still a family and the principles of *11 Reasons Families Succeed* apply to you.

depend totally on God's eternal plan. We did, and we've been doing it that way for almost three decades.

We've seen couples make resolution after resolution to start over, or try harder, only to fail again and again. You and I can try hard, but enthusiasm doesn't compensate for ignorance. If we're "trying hard" with the correct information, then our chance of success is greatly increased. Success comes from obedience to God's system, not from our wisdom or personal efforts. The lack of success in American families and marriages is a direct result of the lack of knowledge of God's Word, and an inadequate understanding of God's plan for marriages and families. God wants you to succeed, but you must know what He says, obey Him, and trust His Word, as you apply each principle to your personal circumstances to produce His intended result. Trust is the key. Your behavior is directly tied to your trust. You must be willing to trust Him with confident obedience in each principle.

There are several truths about marriage and divorce that we will attempt to teach. Here are a few:

## DIVORCE IS EVERYONE'S BUSINESS.

We once overheard a couple in a restaurant telling friends, "Yes it's true, we are getting a divorce, but it really isn't anybody's business."

The failure of a marriage, and the ensuing family difficulties has a ripple effect, which can impact every citizen of our country. It must concern us all because it touches us all.

## DIVORCE IS AMERICA'S BUSINESS.

The foundations of our society are in crisis due to the breakup of the American home. Perhaps you have seen old pilings under a pier that have begun to decay and break apart. The pier itself will lose stability and eventually come tumbling down unless the pilings are repaired. American marriages and families, the institutions that form the foundation of our society, are in much need of repair.

## DIVORCE IS GOD'S BUSINESS.

God is vitally concerned with the state of our marriages and families. Marriage was the first institution He sanctioned and blessed. His great love and plan for mankind centers on men and women committed to Him first, then to each other. As we read the Word, we see how important the family is to God. When families fail, God's perfect plan for a stable society is threatened to the very core.

## WE DON'T HAVE MARRIAGE AND FAMILY PROBLEMS; WE HAVE PEOPLE PROBLEMS.

According to a Gallup Poll released in 1997, the most common reasons for marital breakups are as follows:

- Physical Abuse 5%
- Alcohol and Drugs 16%
- Infidelity 17%
- Incompatibility 74%

Incompatibility simply means that people don't know how to handle their differences, don't know how to handle conflict constructively, and don't, or refuse to, meet each other's needs. In other words, people struggle with the mechanics of relationships. The little day-to-day things trip them up. In this book we will offer suggestions and potential solutions as to how to deal with those daily "little things."

May couples have remained legally married even though they experienced an emotional divorce long ago. Add to this issue the fact that more couples are cohabitating than ever before. Households headed by unmarried partners have increased by 865 percent in the last forty years. In Quebec, Canada, women are even being discouraged from taking their husband's last name. The reason? It is too expensive to change government records if a couple divorces — and of course, the custom of taking the husband's last name violates modern philosophy.

*Nothing becomes depraved in a moment.*
*—JUVENAL*

> *Let thy fountain be blessed: and rejoice with the wife of thy youth.*
> *—Proverb 5:18*

In today's culture, the word "family" is in need of redefinition. The archetype of both parents living in a home with minor children is becoming more and more rare. According to the 2000 U.S. Census, only 23.5 percent of American households are "traditional" families. That is down from almost 51 percent in 1960.

While the single-parent family is most definitely a family, God's perfect plan for the family has not changed. Children are healthier when both mom and dad are there and are committed full time to the family.

We've chosen to include discussions of marriage, child rearing, and the whole gamut of "nuclear family" issues in this study. Our reasons are simple. The parents' marriage impacts the whole family in a dramatic way. Children and their behavior impact the parents' marriage significantly. It's important to realize that whether you are a single parent, separated, married, or a family caregiver, these principles apply to you as well.

## MARRIAGES DON'T FALL APART OR COME APART. THEY DRIFT APART.

We've all been surprised when we heard about the divorce of a couple that seemed perfect for each other. We thought they had a model marriage and family. What could have happened?

Maybe you're in the same situation today. Years have passed, and your dreams and expectations of a wonderful marriage with a loving spouse and great kids haven't materialized as you had planned.

The important thing is to take action when you realize you and your spouse have drifted apart. Our prayer is that God will use these lessons to redirect, refresh, and restore your marriage and family. You can start today. The fact that you hold this book in your hands is an important first step. Don't fail to keep walking step after step through each of the 11 reasons families succeed. And always remember:

## GOD DOESN'T WANT YOUR FAMILY AND MARRIAGE TO "WORK;" HE WANTS THEM TO SUCCEED!

**RICHARD AND RITA**

*The Americans are the hope of the world; they should become its model.*
—*ANNE TURGOT, BARONESS OF AULNE IN A LETTER TO DR. RICHARD PRICE MARCH 2, 1778*

# CHAPTER 1

# SUCCESSFUL FAMILIES HAVE REALISTIC EXPECTATIONS ABOUT MARRIAGE

*So shall you know skillful and godly Wisdom to be thus to your life: if you find it, then shall there be a future and a reward, and your hope and expectation shall not be cut off.*
—*Proverb 24:14* AMP

As a senior pastor, I performed the wedding ceremonies for many couples. During the premarital counseling sessions I always directed the same question to each couple: "So you've decided to be married. Well then, for how long do you want me to marry you?" I continued, "Do you want a ceremony for a couple of years of marriage? How about a ten-year knot? How does a five-year job sound to you?"

As you can imagine, many people were taken aback by my questions. Some were a bit offended. Others were simply amused; they understood the point I was trying to make. Yet every answer was the same. "We plan to be married forever!"

Every couple starts out intending to be married forever. It's the desire of their hearts. It's God's desire for them, as well.

Write out Psalm 37:4 and claim it for your marriage:

_____

_____

*Our expectation fails most oft where it is most oft desired.*
—*SHAKESPEARE*

The problem is, most people believe that just being in love is enough to keep their marriage strong and to keep them together forever. But if that's true, why do so many starry-eyed couples end up in unhappy marriages, or in divorce court?

Often it's because neither partner fully understands the unrealistic expectations they might have about their life together, and how these expectations impact their marriage.

*He who began a good work in you will carry it on to completion.*
—*Philippians 1:6*

When conflict develops they quickly become disillusioned and disappointed. They either never knew or have forgotten that a good marriage takes time and effort; that it requires skill, flexibility, patience, determination, and a life-long commitment to each other and to God.

Let's take a look at five expectations individuals often unknowingly have about marriage. We'll discover what each one is, how it can affect a marriage, and what we can do to prevent it from becoming a problem.

## 1. Marriage Will Be the Answer to My Problems.

*If love is blind, then marriage can be a real eye-opener!*

The truth is, marriage can be one of the most challenging human experiences you'll ever encounter. Without basic communication skills and an understanding of the needs of your partner, it can be a nightmare. Marriage doesn't necessarily get easier, but with God at its center it can get *better*! Remember, marriage is not the answer; it's just a whole new set of questions!

Your first and foremost rule for a successful marriage should not be, "I will make sure I am happy in *my* marriage." The rule for a successful marriage must be, "I will become a blessing to my partner in *our* marriage."

*Everyone looks out for his own interests, not those of Jesus Christ.*
—*Philippians 2:21 NIV*

Write down the six characteristics listed in Philippians 2:1-4 and think about how they apply to your marriage.

_____

_____

_____

_____

_____

_____

Which characteristic do you violate most often in your marriage? Why?

_____

_____

_____

There is a huge difference in entering marriage expecting your new mate to meet your every need all of the time and make you continuously happy, and entering marriage with the attitude that you will do everything you can to serve your mate in love.

A marriage requires each partner to give and take, adjust, forgive, and give and take again. In order to get what you want from marriage, you must first learn to give!

Read Ephesians 5:22-24. How does God instruct a wife to treat her husband?

_____

_____

_____

_____

Now read Ephesians 5:25-28. How does God instruct a husband to treat his wife?

_____

_____

_____

_____

Many times people see marriage as a way to escape a bad home life, poor parents, or unsuccessful relationships. They mistakenly believe marriage can be a "cure-all" for depression, anger, and poor communication skills. Against all reason, people charge ahead with the "head-in-the-sand" notion that marriage will somehow fix what has been wrong in their life for years.

One or both individuals might want to marry in order to create a family unlike the one from which they came. But it's unrealistic to believe that marriage in and of itself will be a magic potion that will somehow wipe out all the past learned behavior and negative experiences.

Many times a person needs deep spiritual healing. Only after that healing takes place should marriage be considered. It's a serious error in judgment to think you don't bring who you are, and who you have been, into the marriage relationship.

Marital success is the triumph of godliness and intelligence over imagination and emotion.

*The way of a fool is right in his own eyes: but he that hearkeneth unto counsel is wise.* —PROVERB 12:15

## 2. DIVORCE COULD NEVER HAPPEN TO ME.

*Put on the full armor of God so that you can take your stand against the devil's schemes.*
*—EPHESIANS 6:11 NIV*

Couples in love often have a romantic vision of an ivy-covered cottage surrounded by a white picket fence where all is happiness and warmth within. Many believe the home they establish can be void of any conflict; perfect harmony will rule; and life will be a continual joyride. "We won't have the kind of families we came from," they promise themselves. But this view is extremely unrealistic. Marriage is like life. There are ups and downs, good days and bad days. It is often better to be alone in life than emotionally and spiritually alone in a marriage.

You'll find ten important aspects of marriage listed below. Rank them according to their importance to you. There may be other things that are important to you that are not on the list. If so, turn to the back of the book and list them.

| | |
|---|---|
| Affirmation and encouragement | _____ |
| Communication | _____ |
| Respect | _____ |
| Common interests | _____ |
| Friendship and companionship | _____ |
| Sexual fulfillment | _____ |
| Understanding | _____ |
| Trust | _____ |
| Tenderness | _____ |
| Spiritual bond | _____ |

Pay close attention to the differences in how you and your spouse ranked each aspect. Christian couples often assume that because they're believers they'll be protected from the threat of divorce. But divorce can and does happen to couples that won't protect and guard their relationship and grow with one another. Don't ignore the possibility. Satan will take every opportunity to attack your lack of preparation at this vulnerable point. It is not fatalistic to consider the possibility. It's wisdom that separates good marriages from foolish, unsuccessful ones. When couples realize and admit that without proper planning and protection divorce could happen to them, they can take the steps necessary to avoid it.

One way of protecting your marriage is by acknowledging God. What does Proverb 3:6 tell you will happen when you do?

_____

_____

There are other ways you can protect your marriage from Satan's destruction. Ephesians 6:10-13 tells of one. Write this passage out.

_____

_____

_____

_____

Does God want you to fear divorce? Write Proverb 1:33.

_____

_____

## 3. WE WILL NEVER ARGUE.

There are couples that have tried to tell us they never argue, never disagree, and never experience conflict. We want to ask, "Do you live together in the same house?" Two people in a normal, healthy relationship are going to have differing opinions and occasional conflicts. That's not bad. Conflicts have the potential to create positive momentum in your life if you use them with wisdom and intelligence.

How can conflict create positive momentum? Write Proverb 27:17.

_____

_____

Conflict happens. It's unrealistic to believe that two healthy people with individual goals, dreams, talents, and gifts won't have disagreements. Even couples who have similar personalities, enjoy the same things, and share the same values are going to have some manner of conflict. The issue is not whether or not you will have conflict. It's how you will handle that conflict that is so critical to your marriage, and ultimately, your family.

### WHEN TWO PEOPLE AGREE ABOUT EVERYTHING, ONE OF THEM IS UNNECESSARY.

The first step to making your dreams come true is to wake up.

*Serve one another in love…if you keep on biting and devouring each other…you will be destroyed by each other.*
—*GALATIANS 5:13-15* NIV

The next exercise may take some time, but it deserves your serious consideration. If you're not married, list ten expectations you have of your future spouse. These can be very detailed or very general. For example, "I expect my wife to always meet me at the door with a kiss when I arrive home," or, "I expect my husband to spend weekends at home and not golfing with his friends." If you are married, list ten expectations you had before marriage that you now realize may or may not have been realistic. For example, "I expected my husband to be the spiritual leader of our home," or "I expected my wife to be more of a sexual partner." Make time to read and discuss the lists together. Read Proverb 19:8 before you begin. Anything on the list that causes pain or anger should be discussed in love and understanding.

1._____
2._____
3._____
4._____
5._____
6._____
7._____
8._____
9._____
10._____

Which items on your list are unrealistic expectations? Why? See Proverb 16:11.

_____

_____

_____

Were some motivated by selfishness or immaturity? Be honest with yourself. See Proverb 3:12.

_____

_____

_____

What do Proverbs 3:5-8 say to do about your unfulfilled expectations?

_____

_____

As time passes, your expectations change. What you want from your marriage today might not be what you wanted when you were first married and might not be what you'll want in the future. Discuss the expectations that you have now. Begin the process of coming to an understanding about what your discoveries mean to your marriage and family.

## 4. MY SPOUSE WILL CHANGE HIS/HER BAD HABITS AFTER WE'RE MARRIED.

It's unrealistic to think a wedding ceremony alone will be the catalyst for positive change in any individual. Sometimes a person hides weaknesses during the romantic period of a relationship and continues the deception right up to the wedding day. Then, when the newness wears off and day-to-day reality sets in, they revert to being who they truly are.

Second Peter 2:17-19 describes a person who is hiding weaknesses. According to these verses, how can we recognize this behavior?

_____

_____

_____

Some weaknesses are more serious than others. Individuals who struggle with alcohol or drug addictions need professional counseling and extended periods of recovery before marriage should be considered. Individuals who exhibit unhealthy sexual attitudes or emotional instability are not candidates for a successful marriage, either. Such individuals need "proving" time – a time when necessary growth and genuine change takes place before marriage can be a viable consideration.

Read Proverb 14:29 and Luke 21:19 to discover what you should avoid when making significant decisions like marriage.

_____

_____

## 5. WE'LL WORK OUT OUR SPIRITUAL DIFFERENCES AFTER WE'RE MARRIED.

Spiritual differences can create some of the most difficult and heartbreaking problems in marriage. The most serious occurs when a believer marries a non-believer. (See II Corinthians 6:14.) Another common difficult situation exists when one partner was reared in one faith and the other was reared in another.

Marriage is not the answer; it's a whole new set of questions.

*Not by works of righteousness we have done but according to His mercy He has saved us.*
*—TITUS 3:5*

*Stand fast in one spirit, with one mind, striving together for the faith of the gospel.*
*—PHILIPPIANS 1:27*

Often, by the time we see a couple in a counseling session, they've already drawn the battlelines and are usually unwilling to change. By then they aren't worshipping anywhere. They know this issue is tearing the marriage and family apart, especially when children are involved.

The conflict and the pain of these situations could have been avoided if, during the dating process, couples had simply discussed and resolved the four basic spiritual issues listed below. Read and determine where you and your partner agree or disagree.

a) Do we share the same basic beliefs about God, Jesus Christ, the Bible, salvation, sin, heaven, and hell?

b) How will we rear our children spiritually?

c) Will church attendance be a part of our lives? If so, which denomination and which church will we choose?

d) Are we committed to being a godly couple from whom our children can learn to emulate spiritual values?

*All spiritual issues should be settled before the wedding or there should be no wedding. It's that important.* An engaged couple that is in tune spiritually should be spending time together in prayer and in the Word. They should worship together and dedicate themselves to rearing their children "in the fear and admonition of the Lord."

Read the following scriptures to discover God's definition of love and what are *realistic expectations* when both partners truly know Him.

Galatians 5:13-15

_____

_____

Realistic Expectation:_____

I John 3:16-18

_____

_____

Realistic Expectation:_____

Ephesians 5:24-25

_____

_____

Realistic Expectation:_____

I Timothy 1:5

_____

_____

Realistic Expectation:_____

Proverb 10:12

_____

_____

Realistic Expectation:_____

I John 3:18

_____

_____

Realistic Expectation:_____


Using Proverbs 4:5, 24:3 as a guide, what specific elements would help build a strong foundation for your marriage and family?

_____

_____

_____

_____

# CHAPTER 2

# SUCCESSFUL FAMILIES KNOW HOW TO PREPARE FOR MARRIAGE

*Which of you, intending to build a tower, sitteth not down first, and counteth the cost, whether he have sufficient to finish it?*
*—Luke 14:28*

Early in our ministry, couples considering divorce came to us for counseling, and we asked certain questions to determine their core problem and help them get their marriages back on track. But it soon became clear we were asking the wrong questions. Now, we begin the first session by asking, "Why did you get married? What brought you together and made you believe you could build a good marriage and family?"

It's amazing how many couples go on for hours talking about what is wrong in their marriage, but have trouble remembering the most important issue: What drew them together in the first place?

When we ask couples why they married, the answer we hear most often is, "We fell in love."

*Well begun is half the doing.*
*—ARISTOTLE*

Many couples don't realize that falling in love isn't the key to planning or preparing for marriage. They enter their marriage as "on-the-job-training" with the hope they can make it work because they fell in love. The truth is, we don't "fall" in love. We grow in love, and love grows in us. That kind of growing love takes a good foundation and preparation.

A popular Captain and Tennille song of the '70s, *"Love Will Keep Us Together,"* had it all wrong. It takes much more than love alone to keep a marriage together – it takes preparation, skill, and a lifelong commitment at the start!

By the time many couples finally come to us, their problems are serious enough to be threatening their marriages. As a result, we find ourselves doing damage control and not much more. So, it's *wonderful* when we hear from a couple that is considering marriage and wants to take the steps necessary to prepare and avoid potential disaster in the future. Sadly, it doesn't happen often. What does happen is, couples will spend thousands of dollars and hundreds of hours planning for a *wedding*, but only an hour or two (if that) with their minister or Christian counselor preparing for the *marriage*.

Benjamin Franklin said it best. "An ounce of prevention is worth a pound of cure." You may be reading this and realize your present family or marriage problems are due to the fact that you and your spouse didn't prepare properly. You didn't add even an "ounce" of prevention to your marriage recipe, and now you need pounds and pounds of cure. Take heart. There is good news. It's not too late to begin again. You can jump-start your marriage by following the six principles outlined in this chapter.

## 1. Marry A Believer.

Maybe you've seen the billboard ad campaign by Bressler Outdoor Advertising. In Milan, Tennesse, simple white letters on a black background proclaim:

## Loved the Wedding,
## Invite Me To The Marriage.
## – God –

It could not have been said better. The One who established marriage and the family wants to be intimately involved in your success, but the is often never invited. You would think this would be, as the teenagers say, "a no-brainer!" If God established marriage, then it is obvious that it takes two who believe in God to make a successful marriage and family. Why would anyone want to marry someone who does not love God? If God is love, then how can you know love if you do not know God?

We've told our children many, many times, *never give your heart to someone who has not first given their heart to God.* This should be the first criteria for a potential mate. If it is not even a consideration, if you leave God out of your relationship, then you are on your own – and that's a dangerous place to be in a marriage. You'll be trying to make your marriage work without following His direction.

God has designed a wonderful plan for a man and a woman in marriage. He set it all in motion. When Christ is at the center of your relationship, He gives your marriage focus, sets priorities, and is the bond that holds the marriage together in rough times. He gives us clear direction in the Bible. Since God is love, unless both partners know God, they cannot know love! Invite Him to help you lay the foundation for a successful family.

Read I Corinthians 13:4-7, then circle the characteristics of love listed below that declare love as a *feeling*. Underline those that portray love as a *way of acting*.

| | |
|---|---|
| Patient | Doesn't keep a record of wrongs |
| Kind | Doesn't enjoy evil |
| Not envious | Rejoices over truth |
| Not boastful | Protects and trusts |
| Not full of pride | Keeps hope alive |
| Not self-centered | Always endures |
| Not quick to anger | |

How many characteristics were feelings? _____

These characteristics of real love are only present in their fullness in individuals who have come to know Christ as Lord and Savior.

*Chance only favors the prepared.*

—Louis Pasteur

When a Christian marries a non-believer, the marriage is immediately in crisis because there is little real fellowship. Tthe Bible calls it being "unequally yoked." The scriptures give a clear directive.

> *Be ye not unequally yoked together with unbelievers: for what fellowship hath righteousness with unrighteousness? and what communion hath light with darkness?*
> —*II Corinthians 6:14-15*

In the period in which the Bible was written, a "yoke of oxen," the term used here to describe marriage, had a traditional meaning. A yoke of oxen consisted of two animals harnessed together by a frame, pulling side by side to plow a straight row in the farmer's field. However, farmers knew that each animal had a "pulling tendency." Some were inclined to pull to the right, some to the left. If the rwo oxen yoked together both had tendencies to pull to the right, the row would be crooked; two left-pulling animals would create the same problem. A good set of animals would include both a "right puller" and a "left puller" in the same yoke. The row would be straight, and the animals' differences would work together to the benefit of both the team and the farmer.

To be equally yoked in marriage involves the same concept. Two individuals take their own unique characteristics and attributes and apply their efforts to their own common goal, a straight furrow in the field. Two believers can share the same goal in marriage of a "straight furrow" in which to plant their dreams and goals. When they allow one another to grow according to the unique attributes each brings to the marriage, they have a great chance to make their family successful.

To be unequally yoked is to purposely choose a marriage relationship that will be marked by misunderstanding, differing values, opposing methods for child rearing, and disharmony.

Many Christians believe that once they are married, the unbeliever will be convinced to become a Christian. Does that ever happen? Yes, in some cases it does, but why take a chance on something this vital to the foundation of a Christian home? Yes, you may have deep emotional feelings for the unbeliever, but this issue, above all others, must be settled before the wedding ceremony. If you're praying that the person you want to marry becomes a Christian, see that prayer answered before you even agree to marry them. God never intended marriage to be an evangelism tool.

Perhaps you have questions as to whether the person you're dating, or a person you're considering as a potential marriage partner, is a Christian. Is a Christian easily identifiable? Read the following verses to clarify genuine salvation, and then put each verse into your own words:

Romans 3:23

_____

Romans 6:23

_____

Romans 5:8

_____

*Love is like a pair of socks; you have to have two and they gotta match.*

*—UNKNOWN*

A great marriage is not two people looking into each others' eyes.  It is two people looking out in the same direction.

Romans 10:9-13

_____

Have you personally taken the steps above that are necessary to being saved? What about your spouse, fiancé, or boyfriend or girlfriend?

A Christian is also recognizable by their lifestyle. They would never embarrass the name of Christ. John 15:5 refers to the Christian as one who "bears fruit." If there is no fruit visible in an individual's life, that person may not be a Christian.

Read the following verses then list some of the "fruit" which is evidence of the Christian life:

Matthew 7:16

_____

Isaiah 57:19

_____

Galatians 5:22

_____

Ephesians 5:9

_____

Proverb 11:30

_____

What if you're already married to an unbeliever? Is there any hope that person will ever come to know Christ? Yes. God honors the prayers and faithfulness of a loving, godly spouse who wants to see their partner come to know Christ. Two particular references in the New Testament should encourage you.

Read I Peter 3:1-2. These verses attest to the hope that an unbelieving husband or wife may be won to the Lord when they observe the life and hear the godly conversation of the Christian wife or husband. Why would the attitude described in verse one be a positive witness and testimony to an unbeliever?

_____

_____

Remember, it's the Holy Spirit Who convicts a person of their sin and draws them to Christ.

According to I Peter 3:4, instead of a critical, judgmental spirit, what kind of spirit should one maintain if they desire their partner's salvation?

_____

_____

Read I Corinthians 7:12-14, then answer the following questions.

Is the believer free to leave his/her unbelieving wife or husband?

_____

First Corinthians 7:14 says the unbeliever is "sanctified" by the Christian spouse. Write what you understand to be the meaning of the word "sanctify." Use a dictionary if it will help you form your definition.

_____

_____

John 17:19 refers to Christ's prayer for us. Fill in the missing words: *And for their sakes I* _____ *myself, that they also might be* _____ *through the truth.*

In Exodus 30:29, God commands Moses to sanctify Aaron and his sons that they may be most holy. This gives us insight into how a Christian can "sanctify" an unbelieving husband or wife. Read the following scripture (John 3:16) as a prayer, inserting your unsaved loved one's name where appropriate:

For You, God, so loved _____ that You gave Your only begotten Son that should _____ believe in Him, then _____ will not perish, but will have everlasting life. Help me sanctify _____ by living a life before _____ that will glorify You so _____ will see the benefit of knowing You and Your Son as Savior and Lord.

# INSPECT THE BAGGAGE

Another element necessary to prepare for marriage is to realize that whether we admit it or not, we all bring "baggage" into a relationship. Our baggage usually consists of past experiences, negative memories, fears, or other issues. This baggage is rarely shared with our partners, and can eventually become the source of great pain and conflict. All baggage should be opened, inspected, and thoroughly examined before the marriage takes place.

Soon after Rita and I married, we found ourselves in a disagreement that led to the discovery of some of our uninspected baggage. In the midst of very heated words, I turned and walked out of the room. I was reared as an only child with an abusive, alcoholic father. I learned to handle conflict by simply walking out. This was part of my baggage; I didn't know how to positively bring conflict to a resolution. When I heard Rita in the other room sobbing uncontrollably from her deep hurt, I returned and asked, "Rita, what's wrong?" Her answer took me by surprise. "Please don't leave in the middle of a conflict. I have memories of my father leaving when any conflict arose at home. Nothing was ever resolved, or healed. Dad's leaving left Mom and us children in great anxiety with questions like, 'Will he be back? What will happen now?' There was never any closure."

Wow! I had no idea that walking away would trigger such painful memories for Rita. She couldn't bear the thought of that negative pattern being repeated in her own marriage.

Until that moment, I wasn't aware of that piece of particular baggage that my new wife had brought into our marriage, and she was unaware of mine. We examined the baggage. We talked about the issue until we both understood it completely. We both had decisions to make. My love for Rita was strong, and I wanted her to feel safe. I assured her that in the future I would not leave during a conflict without some explanation or resolution. She promised to realize that I was not her father and she didn't need to fear abandonment.

Do you know of any baggage that you are bringing, or have brought, into your marriage?

_____

_____

_____

List five aspects about the home and family life you experienced as a child that differ from your spouse's. For example, while your home might have been quiet and stable, theirs might have been loud and often volatile.

*It is smart today to prepare for the wants of tomorrow.*
—*Aesop*

|            YOURS            |        YOUR SPOUSE'S        |
| -------------------------- | -------------------------- |
| _____ | _____ |
| _____ | _____ |
| _____ | _____ |
| _____ | _____ |
| _____ | _____ |

In the space provided below, write your responses to the following statements regarding any areas of baggage that you may need to inspect.

As I was growing up I would have changed the following things about my home life:

_____

_____

_____

Something in my parent's marriage I would like to see in mine is:

_____

_____

_____

Something about my parent's marriage I do not want to happen in mine is:

_____

_____

_____

*He who has begun is half done, be wise and then begin!*

—HORACE, 15 B.C.

Write and discuss with your spouse how the areas described above may affect, or may have already affected your marriage.

_____

_____

_____

_____

_____

It is critical in preparing for marriage that you honestly share any fears, feelings, or behavior related to your past that could cause anger or hurt when revealed later. Inspecting each other's baggage may take some time. It may even require seeking professional help to assist you in dealing with certain baggage belonging to one or both partners.

We've often been asked, "Should I tell my fiancé (or spouse) everything about my past?" That's not always the best decision. You shouldn't feel compelled to "tell all" if you're secure in your relationship, and the person you love has accepted you for who you are now. However, if the information could cause either partner to question the relationship in any way, you must share it. This issue is a difficult one for many people. Our suggestion is, if you are fearful that information will have a negative impact on the relationship or that love or acceptance could be withdrawn, then let love be tested by sharing the information. What is the worst thing that could happen in a premarital situation? The past may be forgiven, understood, and no longer be an issue, or it will be the test of the relationship. If you're unable to share the information because you're afraid, you may never feel the freedom to open up to your partner about any of your shortcomings or weaknesses. If the information can be shared in a loving way, and won't cause undue distress to your partner, then proceed.

*To miss the mark is easy; to hit it is difficult.*

—ARISTOTLE

However, if you're in doubt about confessing to your partner, seek help. Discuss the issue fully with someone you trust. Allow them to advise you as to whether or not you should share the information. If you decide not to do so and then your partner discovers the truth later, explain that you struggled with the decision and did consult with a trusted individual, but thought you were doing the most loving thing by withholding the information. Then ask for forgiveness if this act brought pain to or caused distrust in your loved one in any way.

This is an intensely personal matter. There are no substitutes for the benefits of a clear conscience. If you seriously seek God's guidance, He will reveal the course of action that best suits your situation.

As Christians, we must deal with and then forgive baggage. Because God forgave us, we must forgive others. Write Jeremiah 31:34 as the directive you should follow when your partner reveals baggage to you.

_____

_____

_____

Paul tell us in Philippians 3:13 to forget the things behind us. We are taught through scripture to "forgive one another," but can we actually *forget* a painful experience that causes negative baggage? Write your thoughts about this.

_____

_____

An essential part of a successful marriage is the ability of both partners to ask for and receive forgiveness from each other. According to the following verses why should we forgive?

Ephesians 4:32

_____

James 5:16

_____

II Corinthians 2:10-11

_____

II Corinthians 2:7

_____

Is there anything hindering you or your spouse from giving or receiving forgiveness?

_____

_____

Write a prayer asking God to help you deal with the problems (the baggage) that you or your spouse brought into your marriage. Ask Him to heal and restore your marriage fully.

_____

_____

_____

_____

_____

_____

# SETTLE THE "LEAVE AND CLEAVE" ISSUE

*Therefore shall a man leave his father and his mother, and shall cleave unto his wife: and they shall be one flesh.*
—*Genesis 2:24*

These instructions found in Genesis 2:24 contain two important elements that further prepare us for marriage. In the historical and cultural setting of the Old Testament, it was an understood fact that the woman would leave her parents' home to go live with her husband, so the wording here only includes a directive to the male. But today in our culture, in order to establish a healthy marriage, both partners must understand and follow those clear instructions from God's Word.

## FIRST, BOTH PARTNERS MUST BE WILLING TO LEAVE.

What are we to leave? Each partner much leave the "I" life to take on the "we" life. That takes a major change in thinking and feeling. You must leave anything or anyone that will keep you from becoming totally one with your spouse. You must break all ties with past lovers; you must leave your mother, father, sisters, and brothers.

Emotionally, you're no longer tied to the past – you leave behind your previous identification and behavior as a single person. You leave friends who once held the place of priority in your life. You leave the former practice of thinking of yourself first. You leave everything for the purpose of cleaving to another human being as never before. That decision will form the very foundation of your marriage.

*We do not do what we ought, but we are still responsible for who we are.*

*—ANONYMOUS*

A young bride once came to us who struggled with the fact that her husband never actually left his parents' family to begin his own. He spent more time at his parents' home after he married than he had before. He was so emotionally dependent upon his parents that he called them every day. Every decision the couple made was first sanctioned or approved by her husband's parents. In disagreements, he always sided with his parents instead of his wife. One of his most damaging behaviors was the way he involved his parents in the couple's arguments and turned to them to support his position. He never did leave his parents, as the Bible instructs, to *cleave* to his wife.

Many men and women have the same tendency to hold on to their former lives after they have chosen to marry. There must be leaving before there can be cleaving.

Read Genesis 2:24, which states that marriage is "leaving" and "cleaving." Can you see areas in which you could improve for the benefit of your marriage? List things you should leave in order to cleave more to your spouse. If you've already dealt with this issue, what were some of the more difficult areas you had to leave behind in order to cleave to your new spouse?

_____

_____

_____

_____

## SECOND, BOTH PARTNERS MUST CLEAVE TO EACH OTHER.

The word "cleave" means to lean toward, or be joined to your partner. To cleave to your marriage partner means to choose your spouse above others, even yourself. You cleave, lean toward, or join to your partner by meeting their needs, hearing their words, understanding their feelings, and desires. Together you present a united front to all outside your marriage.

*Life grants nothing worth having to us mortals without hard work.*
*—HORACE, 8 B.C.*

The first Christmas after our son married, we didn't hang his Christmas stocking on our mantel where it had hung the previous twenty-three Christmases. We wanted that simple act to demonstrate to him and his new wife that we understood she was now first place in our son's life. He now had another family, another life, and his own mantle on which to hang his stocking. We believe it helped our new daughter-in-law form an even closer relationship with us by reinforcing the importance of our son's leaving us to cleave to her.

Sometimes parents can impede this clear directive of Scripture by refusing to let go and allow their married son or daughter to build a life apart from them. Each partner is responsible for firmly but lovingly setting limits on the demands of his or her own parents.

It shouldn't be your spouse's responsibility to confront an intruding in-law who is allowed to be too controlling and involved your marriage.

Perhaps you feel that your in-laws or your own parent(s) have knowingly or unknowingly intruded into your marriage. Use the space below to describe your feelings in this regard. Share honestly with your husband/wife. Decide together what can be done and ask God to give you wisdom and the courage to follow-through.

_____

_____

_____

When you cleave to one another in marriage you choose to be one with each other in every way. Scripture gives us four compelling reasons to cleave to each other in marriage. The first is found at the end of Genesis 2:24. It's the command to "be of one flesh," which suggests physical, or sexual intimacy.

**You cleave to each other alone for physical fulfillment and enjoyment.** Read Genesis 2:23, which records Adam's first words upon seeing the woman that God created. Adam said the woman was "bone of my bone" and "_____ of my _____."

We can now more clearly understand Paul's admonition in Ephesians 6:28-29. Read these verses and answer the following questions:

How should a man love his wife?

_____

_____

What does a man love if he truly loves his wife?

_____

_____

What does the man do for his wife that mirrors what God does for the church?

_____

_____

_____

Describe how becoming "one flesh" is a picture of sexual intimacy in marriage.

_____

_____

_____

Adultery violates the exclusive marital sexual relationship. Read Proverbs 6:32 to discover the consequence of adultery, then write the verse.

_____

_____

You not only become one flesh when you cleave to one another, **you also become one mind** – each seeking to understand and honor the thoughts and ideas of the other. This doesn't mean that one partner becomes a mindless robot, mimicking only what the other thinks or feels. It simply means that you have a common purpose, core values, and the same focus for your lives.

Read Romans 15:5-6. Write your answers to the following questions.

What does God grant you so that you may be like-minded?

_____

Why should we seek to be like-minded?

_____

_____


**You cleave to each other to become one in heart.** You want to be joined with your spouse and feel what they feel. Remember Christ's words in Luke 12:34: *"Where your treasure is, there will your heart be also."* It's imperative that married couples treasure the same things, most importantly faith and hope in Christ. Then and only then will they be one in heart.

Read the following verses that refer to the New Testament concept of "singleness of heart," then describe the married couple that demonstrates a "singleness of heart."

Acts 2:46, 4:32, 11:32; Colossians 3:22

_____

_____

_____

_____


**You cleave to your partner in order to be one in spirit.** Being one in spirit is only possible when both have come to know Christ as Savior and Lord. Believers will have different personalities, different gifts, and different callings, but as Ephesians 4:4 proclaims, they will operate in the power of one spirit. Sharing that same spirit will give your marriage vitality, power, and instruction unavailable to unbelievers.

Isaiah 11:2 describes what Christ possessed because of the divine Spirit resting upon Him. Believers, as partakers of this divine nature (II Peter 1:4) share this same wonderful Spirit. Therefore, when two believers marry they truly become one in the Spirit and bring to the marriage all the benefits the Spirit made available to Christ. From Isaiah 11:2, list below six gifts of the Spirit that are the foundation for a godly marriage and home:

_____

_____

_____

_____

_____

_____

# TAKE YOUR TIME

The fourth step in preparing for marriage is to make sure you have spent enough time in preparation. As Shakespeare wrote in *King Henry,* "A hasty marriage seldom proveth well." It takes time to know another person well enough to decide to spend your life with them.. Proverb 21:5 says it well, *"The plans of the diligent and informed will lead to abundance, but every one who is hasty will only come to want and ruin."* A wedding is a one-day event, but a marriage is a lifetime commitment. Take the time necessary to learn everything you can about the person with whom you plan to spend a lifetime.

Couple should focus on two key areas when taking their time to get to know one another.

## GET TO KNOW THE OTHER PERSON'S FAMILY.

Perhaps you have made the mistake of thinking the other person's extended family doesn't matter. The fact is we don't marry one person; we marry, or join ourselves to, the entire family. You must meet the potential in-laws and other family members and spend time getting to know them. Observe how they interact with each other. An old adage fits very well here: An apple doesn't fall far from the tree. This family reared your potential mate, so you need to know who they are and what they believe. Only time can provide answers to the following questions, which you must answer.

- Do you know for certain his/her family's values or habits?
- Is there a spiritual focus of the family? If so, what is it?
- What do they enjoy doing? What are they hobbies and interests?
- How do they handle conflict? How is conflict resolved?

- What is the financial philosophy of the family? Is money important? Is it too important? Did the parents train him/her to be financially responsible?
- How would they react should you choose to marry their son/daughter?
- What kind of in-laws would they be? Uninvolved? Obtrusive? Supportive?
- What was the parenting style of his/her parents? Strict? Flexible? Were they too permissive as parents?
- What kind of influence would they have on your children?

## GET TO KNOW AS MUCH AS POSSIBLE ABOUT HIM/HER.

It will take time to see how the person with whom you are considering marriage handles conflict, jealousy, or failure. Ask any married couple and they will tell you that even when you think you know your spouse there are still many surprises after you are married.

Ideally it's beneficial to see a potential marriage partner in every kind of situation before marriage. To do that will take some time, but it's time well invested. You must observe how he/she reacts in anger, under stressful situations, and in difficult times. It's wise and necessary preparation for a successful marriage to learn about the other person's needs, likes, dislikes, quirks, habits, particular weaknesses, and strengths.

When is the person not right for marriage? We have included some relational warning signs. Some of these characteristics are only revealed over time.

- Is often caught lying.
- Tends to blame others for everything.
- Is cruel to the innocent and weak. This person may be racist.
- Is controlling. Checks up to see where you go, who you are with, etc. Interrogates you if you're late or not home. Insists you get permission from him/her before you go anywhere, etc. Handles all the money.
- Attempts to isolate you from your family or friends. Doesn't want you meeting other people – says he/she is protecting you from people who are not good for you.

- Is extremely jealous. Shows up unexpectedly, checks your phone, even your car mileage. Gets angry if you spend time with anyone other than him/her.
- Quickly says he/she loves you and pushes for serious involvement. Immediately wants an exclusive commitment from you.
- Becomes moody and hypersensitive. Is easily offended. You find yourself constantly apologizing for hurting her/his feelings.
- Verbally berates or attacks you, curses often, is critical, hurtful, or degrading.
- Pressures you for sex. Tries to make up with sex.
- Is repentant but blames for you for his/her actions
- Has pushed, shoved, slapped, or become otherwise physically violent with you.

If any of these characteristics are apparent run, and run fast! The person is not marriage material.

Many people ask us about an ideal period of time for an engagement. Our answer is simple – the length of engagement should be for as long as it takes both parties to feel comfortable about committing for a lifetime. For some that's two years; for others it's only six months. Remember. It is for a lifetime. Think about it. A lifetime!

# ESTABLISH A "COVENANT" MARRIAGE

The fifth step in preparation for marriage is to agree to make your marriage a covenant marriage. Today's so called "modern thinkers" who view marriage as nothing more than a legal contract beneficial to both parties are a real threat to successful marriages.

Marriage is not just a good business deal. You're not building a house that you plan to sell someday for a good profit. God wants your marriage to be more than a legal agreement; He expects it to be a *sacred covenant*. A contract, by its very nature, anticipates that one of the parties may violate the terms. It assumes the worst. This is not the plan God had in mind for any marriage. The following chart lists some differences for your consideration.

The problem is, marriages, children, and families just seem to happen to us and we don't really know how or why.

| Contract | Covenant |
|---|---|
| Based on fear and distrust – is expected to be broken | Based on trust and spiritual commitment |
| Conditional to terms | Unconditional |
| Legal and binding by man's law and standards | Legal and binding by spiritual laws of God and Scripture |
| Usually formed for only a limited period of time | Formed to be permanent and last eternally |
| Exists to protect oneself from the other party | Exists for the benefit of other party |
| Based on worldly principles | Based on scriptural principles |
| Based on selfishness | Based on love (I Corinthians 13:4-7) |
| An agreement before men | A vow before God |

To understand more fully the meaning of covenant marriage we have only to study the origin of the word, "covenant," and how it first appeared in Scripture. With whom did God establish the first covenant? (Genesis 6:18)

_____

The word covenant means to "cut." The term "blood covenant" originated as many of the Old Testament covenants or vows were sealed with blood when skin was cut and blood mingled to attest to the agreement. The term was also used when sacrifices were made as atonement for sins, as in Exodus 24:8. Often you will hear the Old Testament referred to as the Old Covenant and the New Testament as the New Covenant. Of course, the most perfect picture of the New Covenant is when Christ cut a covenant on the cross with His own blood in order to purchase our salvation forever. The word "covenant" appears fourteen times in the book of Hebrews. To give you a clearer understanding of the new covenant, read the following verses in Hebrews, and circle the word covenant each time it appears:

Hebrews 8:6-10, 13
Hebrews 9:1, 4
Hebrews 10:16, 29
Hebrews 12:24
Hebrews 13:20

With the establishment of the New Covenant, vows between Christian men and women in marriage are more sacred and more binding because they involve a vow made not only to each other but also to God. Remember, the most important observer during the wedding vows is not the crowd gathered behind the couple, or the bridesmaids and groomsmen standing with them. It's God. The couple is making their vows publicly before God as the most important witness. They will have to answer to Him should anything happen.

*She's got gaps, I got gaps; we fill each other's gaps!*

—ROCKY BALBOA

Complete the following verses regarding vows.

Deuteronomy 23:21: *When thou shalt vow a vow unto the Lord thy God, thou shalt not slack to pay it: for the Lord thy God will surely require it of thee; and it would be _____ in thee.*

Deuteronomy 23:23: *That which is gone out of the lips thou shalt keep and perform, even a freewill offering, according as thou has vowed unto the Lord they God, which thou hast _____ with thy _____.*

Perhaps you're a married couple that, after reading these verses would like to now establish your marriage as a covenant marriage. Maybe you're a couple who plans to wed and wants your wedding vows to include covenant marriage vows. You can write your own vows or use the vows we've included at the back of this book. We've included a form for married couples as well as a form for couples who plan to be married. God bless you in this decision to invite God to be intimately involved in your marriage for the rest of your lives. A crucial part of the wedding ceremony is the statement at the conclusion, "What God has joined together let no man put asunder." We say, "Yes, and amen!"

# SEEK BIBLICALLY-BASED PREMARITAL COUNSELING

A critical step in preparing for marriage is to find a qualified Christian person or couple to meet with you, mentor you and your fiancé, and help guide you through the engagement period. It doesn't have to be a professional counselor. Many churches have trained individuals who volunteer their services as an outreach of the church. You may know a godly couple that has demonstrated a successful marriage and family. Ask them for their time. You'll be surprised at how honored they will be that you would ask, and how quickly they will agree to work with you. Many pastors require premarital counseling as a prerequisite to a ceremony being held in the church or a ceremony that they will conduct.

Michael McManus stated, "Only one in sixteen marriages in our country experience pre-marriage counseling."[1] That's an interesting statement in light of our divorce statistics. If we will seek professional help when we need new eyeglasses or have a need for surgery, why don't we also seek godly professional counsel and direction as we prepare for marriage?

## WHY IS IT IMPORTANT?

Read the following verses and answer each question.

Psalm 1:1: What will you be when you seek godly counsel instead of ungodly counsel?

_____

Proverb 8:14: What three things do you gain by good counsel?

_____

Proverb 11:14: What happens when people don't receive counsel?

_____

Proverb 15:22: Without good counsel what happens to our purposes?

_____

Proverbs 19:20: What do we become as a result of counsel and receiving instruction?

_____

Amos 3:3 asks an important question: _Can two walk together, except they be agreed?_ It's imperative that couples agree on the principles which will be a part of their marriage before they begin their walk of a lifetime together.

_Nothing can be created from nothing._

—LUCRETIUS CARUS, 55 B.C.

# CHAPTER 3

# SUCCESSFUL FAMILIES UNDERSTAND THE DIFFERENT NEEDS OF MEN AND WOMEN

*In honour, preferring one another.*
—*Romans 12:10*

After over twenty-five years of marriage I (Rita) still marvel over how different Richard and I are. Take, for example, the simple task of ordering food at a restaurant. It drives Richard crazy that I cannot decide quickly what I want from the menu. He believes waiters earn their tip by just taking my order! Also, the things that excite my husband constantly surprise me. Richard loves to head for the office early and stay up late, diving into the details, working for hours on end while I am climbing the walls after just a little while. It is difficult for me to focus on one thing for an extended period of time. I have to have diversity and long breaks to accomplish my work. Our differences caused conflict early in our marriage until God taught us to understand and appreciate our differences. It's not always easy. Let's face it. Because of the different needs of men and women, including the way they think, feel, work, and play, it will always be challenging to understand each other.

Name two or more ways in which your spouse/fiancé is different from you. They could range from simple annoyances to serious issues that cause tension or conflict:

_____

_____

_____

It should come as no surprise that because men and women are different, their needs are going to be different. The key word in the title of this chapter is, "needs." Every husband and wife have certain specific needs – not things they would like to have, but legitimate needs. A need is defined as an essential thing. It is necessary to a person's health and wellbeing.

Don't marry someone you know you can live with. Marry someone you know you can't live without.

# NEEDS VS. NEEDINESS

It would be helpful to discuss an important issue before going on to examine the needs of men and women. If you're married or in a serious relationship with a *needy* person, you'll find it very difficult to meet their needs. The *needy* person is never satisfied. The more you give, the more they want and the more they demand. Nothing is ever enough. Painful consequences may affect the entire family should you marry a *needy* person. The *needy* person should be encouraged to seek professional help. When counseling or treatment is completed, and enough time has passed to demonstrate that healing has taken place, then and only then should that person consider marriage.

The well-known research psychologist, Maslow, suggested that the needs of human beings are the driving force that determines behavior. The Bible could have been the blueprint for Maslow's observations because Scripture verifies this as well.

Read the following and list the basic individual's need(s) mentioned in each scripture reference:

| | |
|---|---|
| Job 11:18 | We need_____ |
| Psalm 4:8 | We need_____ |
| Romans 12:10 | We need_____ |
| I Thessalonians 5: 13 | We need_____ |

All humans have common needs. However, husbands and wives also have differing needs. In this chapter, we will examine those needs.

## WIVES, YOUR HUSBAND IS NOT YOU!
### HE WON'T THINK LIKE YOU, FEEL LIKE YOU, OR REACT LIKE YOU. NO MATTER HOW INTENT YOU MAY BE IN TRYING TO MAKE HIM LIKE YOU, IT WON'T HAPPEN.

## HUSBANDS, YOUR WIFE IS NOT YOU!
### FORGET ABOUT TRYING TO MAKE HER A CARBON COPY OF YOURSELF. IT'S NOT GOING TO HAPPEN. INSTEAD, BEGIN TO EMBRACE YOUR DIFFERENCES. CELEBRATE THEM, ACKNOWLEDGE THEM, AND EVEN LAUGH ABOUT THEM.

The differences between men and women emerge even before birth when the baby boy's brain is bathed in chemicals that shrink the "tunnel" that connects the two sides of the brain. This tunnel is called the corpus callosum. Its job is to transmit messages back and forth between the two hemispheres of the brain. Men tend to operate out of the reasoning, logical side, *or* the emotional, relational side. A man is capable of using both sides of his brain, but the shrinking of the corpus callosum causes him to operate *most efficiently* in half of his brain at a time.

Women, who didn't experience this shrinkage before birth, have the capacity to function with both hemispheres of the brain at the same time. A woman is more aware of her surroundings, and can multi-task more easily. However, this fact may keep her from focusing on one thing. She is easily distracted. Men can focus more easily on one thing and are more project-oriented. They tend to block out distractions.

With all these wonderful differences men and women are still attracted to one another. Amazing!

This chapter is divided into two sections. First, we'll address the needs of women, then the needs of men. It's important that you read both sections because there is information in each for both spouses.

# THE SEVEN BASIC NEEDS OF WOMEN

*The woman, the organizer.*
—VIRGIL, 19 B.C.

Before we look at the needs of a woman and the scriptural definition of her principle role, we must realize that she was created to be a *completer*, or as the Bible states in Genesis 2:18, a "helpmate" to complete her husband. A woman is a remarkable creature who responds to tenderness and understanding by being a helper and by giving back many times over. The woman who lives a satisfying and fulfilling life is one who is giving, nurturing, and *completing* another human being. She is happiest when she is filling her role as a "completer."

Describe ways in which a woman can *complete* each of the following:

Husband

_____

_____

Her children

_____

_____

Others

_____

_____

## 1. A Woman Needs to Be Treated As Something Precious.

Preciousness may be an old-fashioned word to some. It means to be regarded as valuable, important, and worthy. How does a husband meet this need for his wife? He treasures her. He values her! People take good care of something they treasure. A wife can sense what is truly important to her husband by observing the time he dedicates to that interest. What do you love most? What do you treasure? Many wives question their value when they see their husband's job, hobbies, or friends receiving more attention than they are. The woman who does not feel valued believes she must compete for her husband's attention. As a result, she may struggle with low self-esteem, or even depression.

The woman who is treated as something precious knows beyond a doubt that she is the most important thing in her husband's life. She knows this because he makes time for her. He speaks the affirming, encouraging words she needs to hear. He listens to her, values her opinions, and respects her ideas. He gives her emotional support. He shows his affection.

A woman needs many meaningful touches every day. A meaningful touch does not always have to be a *sexual* touch. Sometimes a woman needs to be touched to sense she is precious and valuable, not simply as a precursor to sexual intercourse. Meaningful touches are those given as an expression of love for the sake of love alone.

If a husband touches his wife only when he is interested in sex, she eventually withdraws in resentment. One young woman explained, "The only time my husband strokes my back or even gives me a hug is when he wants to have sex.

It would be nice for him to sometimes just hold me and make me feel loved and safe in his arms instead of using the act as foreplay. There are times I just want him to touch me because he cares, not because he wants sex."

When I (Rita) was about thirteen years old I spent the night with a friend who was my age. Her father came in from work and plopped down in a living-room chair. My friend, excited to see her dad, ran and jumped onto his lap. I'll never forget her father's reaction. I don't think he realized I was there. He stood up, dumping my friend on the floor, and shouted, "What's wrong with you? Act your age and don't do that again!" My friend was hurt and embarrassed. It had to be a memory not easily forgotten. What she wanted was the affirmation of a brief meaningful touch…a hug. I can still imagine (and almost feel) how his rejection must have hurt. A woman – even a young teenage girl – needs tenderness and physical reassurance. She needs the meaningful touches that daily affirm she is valuable. Women who are treated as something precious are usually confident, happy, and secure.

The most romantic things a husband can do are those things that demonstrate how precious his wife is to him. In fact, that's how a woman would define "romance." Romantic moments, as well as romantic acts, are those designed to make a woman feel especially treasured and loved.

*A woman would run through fire and flood for such a kind heart as his.*

—*SHAKESPEARE, THE MERRY WIVES OF WINDSOR*

Using Ephesians 5:25-33 as a guide, answer the following questions regarding how husbands should treasure their wives.

Describe how Christ's love for the Church is a picture of how a husband should love his wife. (Verse 25)

_____

_____


Christ wants to present the Church as glorious and holy, without spot or wrinkle. Does a husband present his wife in much the same way? How? To whom is she presented? (Verse 27)

_____

_____


How does a man love his wife as his own body? (Verse 28)

_____

_____

_____

How does this verse affirm that the husband is committed to the woman? (Verse 31)

_____

_____

_____

How would the world be attracted to Christ by observing this human relationship between a godly husband and his wife? (Verse 33)

_____

_____

_____

## 2. A WOMAN NEEDS HONESTY AND OPENNESS.

One morning while we were driving to a meeting, we found ourselves following two teenage girls in a small black sedan. On the back of the car, a simple black bumper sticker announced, "BOYS LIE." The bumper sticker succinctly expressed the sentiment of too many women who have become accustomed to the lies of men.

Many men don't intend to blatantly lie. They rationalize their white lies and half-truths, not realizing that the result of their dishonesty is quite serious.

Neither men nor women want a spouse who can't be trusted; but for a woman it's imperative that she be able to trust her husband. A woman *needs* her husband to be a man of his word, respected in the community, and known as an honest, forthright man who will do what he says he will do. A woman *needs* to be able to depend on her husband to keep his word, and she becomes heart-broken if she discovers that her husband has been deceitful in any way.

Jan was a widow at age sixty-four. When her husband died suddenly, she discovered that they were deeply in debt. She was left with no alternative but to seek employment at an age when finding work was difficult. The fact that her husband had deceived her by purposely hiding the debt was a devastating blow to her already-broken heart.

Jan's husband was typical of well-meaning husbands who believe they need to *protect* their wives from the truth. What a mistake! Women suffer most when

*How do I love thee? Let me count the ways. I love thee to the depth and breadth and height my soul can reach.*

—ELIZABETH BARRETT BROWNING.

they learn the truth from others, or discover it on their own. A woman needs to be able to trust her husband to be completely honest and open with her about everything, great or small.

Refer to the scriptures below to complete the sentences regarding dishonesty and lying.

Proverb 12:22. *Lying lips are an* _____ *to the Lord: but they that deal truly are His* _____.

II Thessalonians 2:10. *With all deceivableness of unrighteousness in them that perish; because* _____.

Proverb 19:5. *A false witness shall not be* _____, *and he that speaketh lies shall* _____.

I Timothy 4:2. *Speaking lies in* _____; *having their conscience* _____ *with a hot iron.*

Colossians 3:9. *Lie not to one another, seeing that ye have put off the* _____ _____ *with his deeds.*

I John 2:22. *Who is a liar but he that* _____ *that Jesus is the Christ?*

Revelation 21:8. *The fearful, and unbelieving, and the abominable, and murderers, and whoremongers, and sorcerers, and idolaters, and all liars, shall have their part in the* _____ *which burneth with* _____ *and* _____.

Another area in which a woman needs honesty is regarding a man's feelings and his innermost thoughts.

When a woman's need for honesty and openness is met, she feels she is safe and secure with a man she can admire and respect. She appreciates the fact that her husband is a man of godly integrity, and she is grateful for his reputation as an honest, truthful man.

Memorize Proverb 20:7. *The just man walketh in his integrity: his children are blessed after him.*

## 3. A Woman Needs Financial Stability.

The maternal, nurturing nature of a woman is such that she wants to provide security, peace, and protection for those she loves. To her, financial stability means that her household will be clothed, fed, housed, and cared for. Financial instability produces great anxiety. If there are children, she may fear they will be deprived of their basic needs.

It's important to note that a woman doesn't need wealth or abundance in the form of new cars, the finest clothes, or the most expensive home. What she needs is the feeling of safety that comes when her family's basic needs are met. A woman admires a man who is hard-working, frugal, and determined to meet those needs for his family. One of the most comforting thoughts for her is knowing her husband will do all he can do – work overtime and hold down two jobs if necessary – to provide for his family.

Many men have simply refused to assume their God-given role as the provider and protector for the family. Consequently, women, out of necessity, have had to take on the role. The need for financial stability compels women to do what was originally designed as a godly mandate for the man.

Read I Timothy 5:8. The scripture labels a man who does not provide for his family as "worse than an infidel." Those are very strong words considering the meaning of the word "infidel." Using your dictionary, write down the meaning of the word, "infidel."

_____

_____

_____

In your own words, explain why your not providing for your family is such a serious offense to God.

_____

_____

_____

Financial stress causes many marriages to fail. In your opinion, why is financial stress so detrimental to a marriage?

_____

_____

Read the description of the industrious ant in Proverbs 6:6-11. Verse 6 says we can learn and grow wise by considering the ant's ways. Below, list the ways we can emulate the ant's preparation and diligence to provide for the family.

_____

_____

_____

When a husband meets his wife's need as a provider of financial stability, the wife has her own responsibility. She mustn't overspend or apply undue pressure on her husband for more than they can afford. She must be a partner in trimming costs and watching the budget. Read Proverbs 31:16. Financial stability will bring peace and harmony to a home while meeting the woman's need for security.

## 4. A WOMAN NEEDS A MAN'S COMMITMENT TO THE FAMILY.

A woman needs to know the family is her husband's first priority. She needs her husband to demonstrate his commitment to the family by making time for his family. Too many husbands seem to be more committed to their careers, friends, sports interests, or hobbies because those are what interests consume their attention and time, and the family gets what is left – which is often very little. There's an old adage that is very appropriate: Love is spelled T-I-M-E.

## FATHERS, YOUR CHILDREN WILL HAVE MANY FRIENDS IN THEIR LIFETIME; THEY WILL HAVE MANY TEACHERS AND OTHERS WHO WILL CARE FOR THEM. BUT ABSOLUTELY NO ONE CAN BE YOUR CHILD'S FATHER BUT YOU.

Your children should never have to doubt their father's commitment to his family. You need to show it daily. Be at the ball games; attend every school play or program; be your child's greatest cheerleader. Make time to hear their simplest requests. Nothing will be more important to your children than knowing throughout their lives that their father was committed to the family.

On a personal note, our children still speak of the confidence they had knowing that their dad always made time for them. We made it clear to them they could interrupt my busiest day at any time because they were my most important priority.

*Somewhere she waits, strong in belief, your soul in her firm white hands: thank well when she comes to you, the woman who understands.*
—EVERARD JACK APPLETON, "THE WOMAN WHO UNDERSTANDS"

Read the following scriptures and name the attributes or characteristics of a good father described in each.

Matthew 7:11

_____

Luke 15:20-24

_____

Proverb 1:8

_____

Isaiah 38:19

_____

Psalm 103:13

_____

Joshua 24:1

_____

## 5. A WOMAN NEEDS A HUSBAND WHO IS TEACHABLE.

A wife needs to know her husband is open to counsel. Why would this be a need for a woman? Because one person never has all the answers.

Most women have observed what happens when narrow-minded, inflexible men are unwilling to grow, learn, or change. They know these men feel threatened when asked to adapt or admit error in any way.

*After over a quarter century of marriage, I finally have my wife right where she wants me.*
—*RICHARD TATE*

Wise is the husband who is open to what his wife and children can teach him. A wife wants her husband's success more than anyone else does. She has insights and spiritual and intellectual gifts that can be an advantage to him socially, spiritually, in the workplace, and at home. A secure, self-assured, emotionally healthy man welcomes his wife's counsel and direction. Not only does she not intimidate him, he wants to learn from her. He values her opinions and gains knowledge from her; he sees her gifts as his own strength. A man who is unwilling to be taught doesn't deserve to be a teacher.

The teachable man also is a man who is eager and willing to be taught spiritually. He opens his life to the leadership of the Holy Spirit and longs to grow and become all that God wants him to be. Under the direction of the Word of God, he will be open to change his behavior patterns. He will seek counsel from godly friends when needed. He will be teachable concerning the needs of his wife and family members. He will be the man who always seeks more of God to benefit his life and the lives of his family members. What a blessing to a woman when her husband meets her need by becoming a teachable man!

What does Proverbs 19:20 urge men to do to be wise? *Hear* _____; *receive* _____.

In Scripture, several men were so dramatically changed after being taught and led by God that their names were changed to affirm the spiritual transformation had that occurred.

Read the portions of Scripture below that relate to a man's name being changed after a significant encounter with God. Write his new name and its meaning.

Genesis 17:5: Abraham
New name and meaning:_____

Genesis 32:28: Jacob
New name and meaning:_____

Matthew 16:17-18: Simon Barjona
New name and meaning:_____

According to Proverb 1:5, what will a wise man do?

_____

## A WOMAN NEEDS CONVERSATION.

Women, by nature, tend to be more verbal than men. This characteristic, and a woman's need for information, are the result of a woman's desire to nurture. She believes that if she has enough information, she can determine the safest course for her family. When she knows the facts and has all the details, a woman feels more secure. Women are often perceived as nosy or obtrusive busybodies when

*She is more important to me than all the hundreds of other roses because she is MY ROSE.*
—THE PRINCE TO THE FOX, THE LITTLE PRINCE

actually they are just demonstrating a need for information, words, and conversation.

A woman isn't just being pleasant when she asks her husband or child, "How do you feel?" She really *needs* to know. She appreciates the efforts of her husband and others to meet her need for information and conversation.

On countless occasions we have ourselves observed the differences between our son and daughter in the area of verbalization. When both were away at college, for example, there were many phone conversations; but our son's calls were strikingly brief, while conversations with our daughter were several times longer. Why? It isn't that women are too talkative; they simply have a greater need for conversation and words. The details are important to them.

A woman needs *specific words* from her husband: words of affirmation, love, and encouragement that only a husband should provide. Her self esteem and security are intact when she hears her husband express how he feels about her. The humorous story of the insensitive husband who said, "I told my wife I loved her twenty-five years ago when we got married. If I ever change my mind, I'll let her know," typifies the lack of interest some men have in verbally expressing feelings of romance or appreciation toward their wives or children.

> The very best marriages are the ones in which the chase is never over.

Sadly, extramarital affairs can be birthed when someone other than a woman's husband begins to meet her need for conversation. If a colleague at her workplace or a close male friend provides the conversation, the interest, and the affirmation a woman needs, a woman, even though totally unjustified in her actions, may then find herself becoming emotionally attached and dependent on this man instead of her husband.

Read Proverb 18:21 and describe how a husband's words can be like death or life to a woman.

_____

_____

_____

Complete the following verses to see how a husband can meet his wife's need for affirming, loving words.

Ecclesiastes 10:12. *The words of a wise man's mouth are* _____;
_____

Proverb 16:24. *Pleasant words are as an honeycomb,* _____ *to the soul, and*
_____ *to the bones.*

Proverb 15:1. *A* _____ *answer turneth away wrath: but* _____
*words stir up anger.*

Proverb 15:23. *A man hath* _____ *by the answer of his mouth: and a word*
_____ *in due season, how good is it!*

## 7. A WOMAN NEEDS HER HUSBAND TO BE THE SPIRITUAL LEADER IN THEIR HOME.

When a man abdicates his sacred and God-given role as the spiritual head of his home, a wife often has no choice but to direct the household spiritually. Some women are forced into this leadership role through other circumstances. Many are single moms, widows, or grandmothers rearing children alone. Whatever the situation, a woman's preference is that her household looks to a male role model, a father to imitate and follow. A woman needs a husband who will be a godly example. She needs to have confidence that her husband will be the moral and spiritual leader God intends him to be.

Read Joshua's declaration that as the spiritual head of his home his family would serve the Lord. (Joshua 24:15)

Husband, if you are a Christian and are striving to be the spiritual and moral leader of your home, write your family's declaration of faith below. Single mothers or grandmothers, who have to fill the role of spiritual leader, write your declaration as well.

*As for me and my house we will...*

_____

Share this declaration with your family and ask for their prayers and support as you lead your family spiritually.

A wife yearns for a praying man who desires to obey and love God with all his heart and will teach his family to do the same. Those who suffer most when a man is corrupt or immoral are always his wife and children. A woman who knows her husband loves God, obeys His word, and strives to be God's man in every way has great peace of mind and heart.

If a misguided or immature man believes this God-given designation gives him license to run roughshod over his family's feelings and views, there can be negative results. It displeases God greatly to see a man with an authoritarian spirit producing fear and anxiety in his wife or children.

**IT'S NOT THE RESPONSIBILITY OF A MAN TO SEE TO IT HIS WIFE AND CHILDREN DO WHAT HE SAYS TO DO, BUT THAT THROUGH HIM THEY SEE THE BENEFIT OF DOING WHAT GOD SAYS TO DO.**

Because this need of women for a spiritual head, it is imperative that a woman marry a believer. We are very direct with young women who are considering marriage. To settle for less will mean her need for a moral and spiritual leader in the home will go unmet, and the results could produce generations without spiritual strength and direction.

**THE WORLD DOES NOT NEED MORE MANLY MEN; WHAT THE WORLD NEEDS IS MORE GODLY MEN.**

# THE SEVEN BASIC NEEDS OF MEN

## 1. A MAN NEEDS ADMIRATION AND RESPECT.

Every male from age two to 102 needs to be admired and respected. In fact, a man would rather be admired than loved. What do we mean? When a man is admired, he feels loved. That is the language of love for the male, *words of affirmation and admiration*. Specifically, the man needs his wife's admiration and respect. He may or may not have admiration from his boss, fellow employees, or other family members. He may be in a thankless job where there is little praise or recognition. Yet when he has a loving wife who bolsters his self-esteem by finding things about him to admire, he feels successful.

Ephesians 5:33 states that a woman should revere her husband. Other translations state the woman should be in awe of her husband. In other words, Scripture suggests that wives should look for ways to admire their husbands.

Wives, list at least five things about your husband you admire and respect.

_____

_____

_____

_____

_____

Tell your husband you admire these things about him as soon as possible. Even if you've told him recently, tell him again. After you do, note how he reacted.

_____

_____

One has only to observe the difference in young men who have been criticized, ignored, or berated and those who have been praised and affirmed to see how important affirmation is. Young men who have a steady diet of justifiable admiration and respect grow to be confident, caring contributors to society. The others are programmed to fail because of the lack of support and praise in their lives. When the need for admiration is not met in the home, a young man will seek it outside the home — from gangs, unwholesome relationships, or any other source that will help satisfy that need.

When a woman understands this need, she will realize that the tiniest word of praise and admiration from her will do wonders for a man's ego. His balance is restored and he feels complete and successful when one person, the person he loves most, gives him support and encouragement. Critical words from her are the words which devastate him the most.

Men encounter women daily who are more than willing to meet his need for admiration. Another woman's glowing words of adoration could be the hook that draws a needy husband into sin. Affairs in the workplace are rampant due in part to a husband's needs being met by someone other than his wife. It is the wise and loving wife who learns to meet the man's need for respect and admiration.

Proverbs 5:3-4 describe in dramatic fashion how immoral women use words of admiration and respect to trap men into infidelity.

*As long as you know that most men are like little boys you know everything you need to know about men.*

—COCO CHANEL

*For the lips of a strange woman drop as an* _____, *and her mouth is smoother than* _____.

The verses below instruct a husband to be faithful and committed to his wife alone – not to be swayed by strangers. What is each asking the husband to do?

Proverb 5:15

_____

Proverb 5:18

_____

Proverb 5:19

_____

A wife can see even the physical effects that take place in her husband when she begins to tell him the things about him that she admires and respects. He walks differently, talks differently, and has a new and invigorating outlook on life when his wife loves him enough to meet this important need. Of course, the man must strive to be a man worthy of her admiration and respect.

Many wives withhold words of admiration and respect intentionally, or because they have never been taught the importance of using gracious, loving words to bless another. Proverb 3:27 admonishes us to bless others by word or deed whenever possible. Write out this important verse and commit it to memory.

_____

_____

## 2. A MAN NEEDS SEXUAL FULFILLMENT.

It should surprise no one when we suggest that men are more sexually oriented than women. Women will often offer sex in order to receive intimacy (remember her need is to be treated as something precious), and men will feign intimacy in order to get sex. It is a complex issue, but one that is central to the marriage relationship, and ultimately to the health of the family. God created men to be sexual by nature in ways that women may not understand. For example, a man is more easily stimulated sexually by visual images. The physical release from orgasm is one of the most powerful urges for a man. Wives who misunderstand the sexual needs of their husbands may mistakenly believe them to be too sexual or oversexed. Such a wife may attempt to make her husband feel guilty, accuse him of excessive preoccupation with sex, or suggest that something is wrong with him because of his strong sex drive. But when a woman realizes that sexual fulfillment is a man's *need*, she will be more open to understanding and meeting that need.

Some wives may have to give an account to God for the way in which they belittled or ignored their husband's sexual needs. Many marriages would blossom overnight should the wife decide to embrace this part of her husband's physical and emotional makeup. When a wife begins to genuinely anticipate meeting her husband's sexual needs, romance can be reborn.

Instead, many women dread the sexual encounter and avoid it, using excuse after excuse to postpone it. Of course, this attitude doesn't go unnoticed by the man. He begins to take it personally and his ego suffers. His wife's disinterest may make him feel undesirable. When his sexual needs are finally met, he often feels like he has forced himself upon his wife, and the experience leaves him frustrated and less than satisfied.

The husband in such a situation has a dilemma. He must reconcile the fact that he needs sexual fulfillment, with a price that is too great to pay. He may withdraw physically from the wife, even seeking sexual gratification in pornography or a relationship outside of the marriage.

Psalm 139:14 declares that we are fearfully and wonderfully made. A wife who appreciates that her husband was created with different needs yet is fearfully and wonderfully made, rejoices in those differences. Using verses from the beautiful Song of Solomon, we have given you some areas by which your romantic, sexual episodes can become more fulfilling with just a little forethought. Wives, you may want to add some ideas of your own to demonstrate to your husband that meeting his sexual needs is both an honor and a joy.

• **PREPARE FOR YOUR ENCOUNTER.** Set time aside for intimacy. We lead very busy lives, so planning for intimate times is as important as planning for an evening out or a visit from friends. Wives, your husband knows you've made time to be with him because it's a priority for you.

*Until the day break, and the shadows flee away, I will get me to the mountain of myrrh, and to the hill of frankincense.*
—*Song of Solomon 4:6*

• **PREPARE YOURSELF.** When making love, don't wear the ragged T-shirt you've had since high school. Celebrate this intimate time, and honor your husband by wearing something feminine. Prepare your body – use lotion and understated cologne if so desired.

> *How fair is thy love, my sister, my spouse! how much better is thy love than wine! and the smell of thine ointments than all spices! Thy lips, O my spouse, drop as the honeycomb: honey and milk are under thy tongue; and the smell of thy garments is like the smell of Lebanon.*
> —*Song of Solomon 4:10-11*

• **PREPARE THE PLACE.** Because a man is stimulated by sight, sound, and sensations, use candlelight, fragrance, and soft music to enhance this special time.

> *My beloved is gone down into his garden, to the beds of spices, to feed in the gardens, and to gather lilies. I am my beloved's, and my beloved is mine: he feedeth among the lilies.*
> —*Song of Solomon 6:2-3*

• **PREPARE THE WORDS.** It is very sensual for a man to hear his wife verbally admire his body or to tell him about the things he does that are attractive or appealing to her. Share with him why he is sexually attractive to you and why you are grateful to be his wife. For a hint as to how it's done, read the following passage:

> *My beloved is white and ruddy, the chiefest among ten thousand. His head is as the most fine gold, his locks are bushy, and black as a raven. His eyes are as the eyes of doves by the rivers of waters, washed with milk, and fitly set. His cheeks are as a bed of spices, as sweet flowers: his lips like lilies, dropping sweet smelling myrrh. His hands are as gold rings set with the beryl: his belly is as bright ivory overlaid with sapphires. His legs are as pillars of marble, set upon sockets of fine gold: his countenance is as Lebanon, excellent as the cedars. His mouth is most sweet: yea, he is altogether lovely.*
> —*Song of Solomon 5: 10-16*

• **PREPARE TO TOUCH.** Physical touch is both stimulating and reassuring to the man that you are welcoming the sexual encounter. Through kissing, mutual touching, perhaps even intimate massage, the couple is preparing sensually for intercourse.

> *It was but a little that I passed from them, but I found him whom my soul loveth: I held him, and would not let him go.*
> —*Song of Solomon 3:4*

Perhaps you would like to send a very private message meant only for your spouse. Talk candidly about what would make your sexual relationship more enjoyable and fulfilling for you.

Unresolved sexual problems produce a great amount of friction in marriage. They must be a matter for discussion. Professional counseling is appropriate when couples cannot resolve sexual issues alone.

A woman must be able to communicate with her husband in order for him to be sensitive and thoughtful of her emotional state of mind as well as her physical state. A young wife who has spent the entire day caring for a teething infant and a busy toddler nears the end of the day exhausted and frazzled. She may not feel romantic or sexually inclined at bedtime. For her at that moment, the most loving thing a husband could do would be to draw her a hot bath and offer her a back rub and a soft bed.

A wife must help her husband understand that a woman prefers to give herself sexually when she isn't fragmented, when she can focus on sex as a romantic interlude, and when it feels right. Some men have difficulty relating to the woman's need for this kind of preparation for sex. It has been said that when it comes to sex, women need a reason and men need a place. Although crude, that statement holds a bit of truth about our different approaches to sex. Both need to work to meet each other's needs in this area for pleasurable sexual experiences.

For some women, sexual intercourse may not be pleasurable because of physical reasons. Certainly a physician can help you determine the cause and the treatment in those cases. Don't go on for years without seeking help in this important area of intimacy.

One important area of sexuality is the role of pornography in marriage. Some modern-day counselors advise couples to introduce pornography into their marriage, especially if it is a sexually troubled marriage. However, pornography is not a sexual aid for marriage. It's a form of adultery. It's adulterous because it brings another person into the marriage relationship. That person may be a picture in a magazine, an image on the screen, or a fantasy of the mind. Any time you bring someone else into the exclusive marriage relationship you are involved in adulterous behavior.

It's absolutely wrong to introduce any kind of sexual activity that makes a partner feel uncomfortable or compromised spiritually.

Read Matthew 5:27-28 and summarize it in your own words.

_____

_____

_____

Sexual differences are among the leading cause of marital conflict and misunderstanding. A healthy, successful couple discusses this area thoroughly. They know each other's needs, desires, and limits.

## GOD IS PLEASED WHEN A WOMAN EMBRACES THE FACT THAT HER HUSBAND HAS BEEN CREATED TO NEED SEXUAL FULFILLMENT, AND FEELS HONORED TO BE THE ONE TO MEET THAT NEED.

Wives, begin to anticipate that sacred intimate time and minister to your husband by approaching the sexual encounter not as a duty, but as a joy and a privilege. Read I Corinthians 7:2-4, preferably from *The Living Bible*, then complete the following questions.

According to verse 3, what should we give each other in marriage?

_____

Verse 4 states that a married woman no longer has full rights to her body, for her husband now has rights to it as well. The same applies to the husband's body. What happens when we refuse these rights to each other?

_____

_____

Read Hebrews 13:4. With the help of a good Bible commentary, explain the statement, *"Marriage is honourable in all, and the bed undefiled...."*

_____

_____

_____

## 3. A MAN NEEDS A PEACEFUL HOME.

We live in a chaotic world in which we are bombarded daily with pressures from every direction. Many men have highly stressful jobs where the pace is often frantic and harried. Yet many men leave a stressful work environment only to return to an equally stressful environment when they arrive home. Men need a refuge, a safe place. Ideally, that place is his home. A man needs his home to be the one place that is not chaotic, but where things make sense and there is order. He doesn't need a perfect home, just a sense of normalcy in a place where things are the way they are supposed to be.

It's important to note that today many women work outside the home and experience equal amounts of stress and demands on her time. We do not propose that it is the wife's responsibility alone to create a peaceful home. We are simply stating here that it is important that a wife understand the man's genuine need for peace and order.

The peaceful home is sometimes noisy with the happy chatter of children. There might be clutter in the entryway or on the stairs. The peaceful home can be made up of children, teenagers, and parents who have problems, *but they are not out of control.* There is a calm center, a focus. God rules this home, and it is bathed in love and prayer.

The wife who wants to help create a peaceful home should make it a habit to allow her husband to *come home.* By that, we mean to give him some time everyday to unwind. There will be time later to fill him in on why Johnny needs discipline, or why the dental bill is so high, but for a few moments after he arrives, allow your husband to really come home. He will appreciate the opportunity to change perspectives, to switch hats from the dog-eat-dog corporate world to the world of warmth and caring that his home should provide for the whole family.

Again, it is not the responsibility of the wife alone to create a peaceful home, but she does have a lot to do with the spirit of the home. The wife is the heart and emotion of the home. If she is an angry, bitter, or complaining woman, the temperament of the home will be the same.

Proverb 21:19 states it is better to live where? than with an angry, complaining woman. _____.

According to Proverb 27:15, a woman who is continually whining and complaining is like _____.

A sullen, moody woman creates a home that others will want to avoid. It will not be a place where others feel welcome and comfortable.

Of course, the man also contributes greatly to the home's personality. I (Rita) remember when our children were small and it was time for Daddy to come home. It was a happy time of day. They would run to walk Daddy into the house, take his coat, and sit him down in his favorite chair. Daddy brought peace into our home, not discord or havoc.

Many children run from the presence of their father when he comes home. They know that Daddy is usually tired and angry, so they dive for cover when he comes through the door. A father's presence in the home should signal safety, provision, and guidance, never fear and anxiety. A man *needs* a peaceful home even when he is the one whose spirit and attitude may make it otherwise. As world events become more chaotic, and unrest and violence seem to darken the horizon, our homes can be "places of light." Write Exodus 10:21-23 in your own words.

_____

_____

_____

*Woman is the very soul of a man.*
—Don Quixote to Aldonza

## NO MATTER HOW DARK THE WORLD BECOMES, YOU CAN HAVE LIGHT IN YOUR DWELLING!

In addition to meeting the man's needs for a peaceful home, such an environment allows our homes to be testimonies of God's presence. Below are seven verses, which affirm the kind of Christian home we can have through

Christ Jesus. Read each reference, then write the word from that verse that best describes the kind of place our homes should be.

Acts 7:33

_____

Isaiah 32:18

_____

Psalm 32:7

_____

Ephesians 4:32

_____

James 5:16

_____

Deuteronomy 26:2

_____

Psalm 144:15

_____

Is your home a happy place or a heavy place? A man who has a peaceful, happy home will be a better employee, be healthier, live longer, and have greater emotional balance.

## 4. A Man Needs a Wife Who Cares About Herself.

A man doesn't need a wife with a perfect figure or the most beautiful face. But a man does need a wife who cares about herself – the way she looks, her clothes, and her personal habits. In other words, it is important to him that his wife strives to be as attractive as she can be. In our society, appearance is important – too important. However, it remains true that often the first impression lands the job, opens the door, or makes the sale. A wife is an extension of her husband. Others perceive her as a reflection of his leadership, his values, and his priorities. Therefore, a husband appreciates a wife who is self-assured, attractive, and content.

The most attractive women are not always the ones who have the most pleasing physical characteristics. It is the woman who has a beautiful spirit, gentle voice, and easy smile that we think of as most attractive.

We mustn't overlook the fact that the reason many women don't care about being attractive is because their own needs go unmet. They're unhappy, insecure women. The wise husband who meets his wife's need to be treated as something precious will see how she blossoms under such unconditional love.

We've all met the woman who appears beautiful physically but whose attitude or personality makes her very unattractive. Godly women have an inner beauty that radiates love and warmth and produces an outer beauty that is most attractive. A man needs his wife to strive to be the godly, beautiful woman described in I Peter 3:3-4. According to this scripture, what adornments make a woman most beautiful?

_____

_____

*Men* – What do you find most beautiful/attractive about your wife? Use the space below to list the reasons that she meets this need for you. Share your list with her as soon as possible.

_____

_____

_____

_____

_____

## 5. A MAN NEEDS A WIFE WHO IS HIS CHEERLEADER.

This is different from the man's need for admiration and respect. A man needs a cheerleader even when he hasn't done anything for which he deserves admiration. He needs one person – his wife – to be there for him even when he has failed, or has just had the worst day of his life. He needs a wife who will love him, be on his side, and encourage him when all others have given up or don't care.

Our daughter, Trinity, was a cheerleader for the University of Oklahoma during a rebuilding year when they were struggling to win football games. During one particular game, Oklahoma was down by four touchdowns with only a few seconds left in the game. There was Trinity, still cheering, still encouraging, still pumping up the crowd, and still believing her mighty Sooners would be able to pull out a miracle victory with "Sooner Magic." She was doing what a cheerleader does. Cheering!

Every husband needs a wife who will be his cheerleader, even when he is losing, or when he has already lost, whether he has had a good game or a bad game. When a man is having trouble believing in himself, he needs a wife who will believe in him. Such a wife is a treasure.

Proverbs 31:10-31 is the discourse honoring the virtuous woman. These verses refer to a wife who builds up her husband and family by encouraging them. She's their cheerleader! See:

Verse 11 – What does the heart of her husband do?

_____

Verse 12 – What does the wife do for a lifetime?

_____

Verse 25 – What are her clothes?

_____

Verse 28 – What do her children and husband call her?

_____

*"This is it!" Adam exclaimed. "She is part of my own bone and flesh."*
—GENESIS 2:23 TLB

Several years ago we experienced a huge business failure. Overnight we suffered a devastating financial loss. I (Richard) had failed by making ill-advised decisions. It was a very emotionally draining, difficult time. Rita gathered the children around and told them the situation. She said it would be hard for the next few weeks, and that we would have to change some of our spending habits – and that Dad was feeling pretty low. She organized the children to help her plan a special dinner for that evening.

When I came in from work, Rita and the children stood up around the table that was already prepared for dinner. They applauded and cheered as I entered and took my place at the table. Rita said, "We just wanted you to know we believe in you, and no matter what happens we are in this thing together. You are not alone. We know God will see us through because you are a wonderful man. You are the wisest, strongest man we know and we love you." Then they cheered some more. It was a night none of us will ever forget.

I thank God for a wife who is a heaven-sent cheerleader for me and who has taught my children to be the same. I had new hope, a positive perspective, and a renewed confidence that I could go on. I didn't deserve it, but I definitely needed it. Rita had every right to say, "I told you so." But she didn't. She was my cheerleader, and the success which came in the years which followed would not have happened had it not been for her skill, insight, Godliness, and understanding of my needs.

Read Ephesians 4:29. It instructs us to speak only that which is good to edify or lift up others. In this way, the verse says, we minister grace to those we love by being a cheerleader for them.

Wives, express to your husband that you realize that this is a need you want to meet for him, and then ask him how you can be more of a cheerleader for him.

What can you say or do today that would show your husband that you are his cheerleader?

_____

*I know you say you love her, but do you like her? Loving is a wonderful thing but liking is the most important thing.*

—JIMMY STEWART,
"SHENANDOAH"

Perhaps you need to ask his forgiveness for a time when you were not. Recall it here.

_____

Fill in the words below from Ecclesiastes 4:10 that encourage us to lift up those who may have fallen.

*If they fall, the one will lift up his fellow: but woe to him that is alone when he falleth; for he* _____.

Below are just a few "cheerleader" phrases that a wife can use to bless her husband. Speak them every day.

- I'm so proud of you.
- I knew you could do it.
- You really make my day.
- You are so responsible.

- Wow! You did it.
- I love you.
- I appreciate how hard you try.
- You are a joy to me.
- I trust you totally.
- You make me feel so safe.
- You are so gifted.
- Way to go!
- Thank you for being such a good listener.
- I am praying for you.
- You're the best!

Your commitment, both husband and wife, to be each other's cheerleaders will get you through rough days, encourage your children, and be the cause for great celebration in your home as you support and honor each other.

## 6. A Man Needs a Wife with a Sweet Spirit.

A woman can possess either a sweet spirit or a bitter spirit. She can be controlling or submissive. She is either content or dissatisfied. A man needs a sweet-spirited woman who lives in love, not selfishness. A man needs his wife to be understanding and flexible, not given to mood swings and childish tantrums.

Several years ago we were dining with a pastor and his wife at a very nice restaurant. The pastor was a kind and attentive man; however, his wife became so belligerent and rude to the waitress that we were all very embarrassed – the pastor had to be most embarrassed of all. We didn't presume to know why the wife had such an angry demeanor; we just know that her critical attitude was not a blessing to her husband. A man needs a wife who will be a blessing to him and others – a woman with a sweet spirit.

Instead of telling our daughter she was beautiful, we would often tell her how much we loved her sweet spirit. She is indeed a stunning young woman physically, but we wanted to reinforce that the most important thing was her inner beauty. Read Proverbs 31:30 and write it in your own words.

_____

_____

How do you recognize a woman with a sweet spirit? What does she possess, according to I Peter 3:4, "...which is in the sight of God of great price?"

_____

From Ephesians 5:1-4, list some of the characteristics that mark the life of the sweet-spirited woman.

_____
_____

*A day without you is like a day without honey.*

—Winnie the Pooh

The woman who possesses a sweet spirit knows that she is precious to God and realizes her value to her husband and children. Proverbs 31:28 declares that her children and husband rise up and call her _____.

Such a woman is an example of the believer in six ways listed in I Timothy 4:12. Write them here.

_____
_____
_____
_____
_____
_____

The sweet-spirited woman is most fulfilled when she is being what she was created to be, a godly woman, the completer of her husband and children, a helpmate. But you can't just determine to be a good woman and possess such a spirit. This spirit is only possible through the indwelling of the Holy Spirit. Read I Peter 1:22.

_____
_____

## 7. A MAN NEEDS HIS WIFE'S RADAR.

Successful men have an asset that helps to complete them and give them extra insight in every area of their lives. That miracle ingredient is his wife's intuition, or "radar" as we like to call it. When a man is willing to be influenced by his wife's intuitive gifts he will benefit greatly. A man needs his wife's radar because she can usually be more discerning of people's motives, as in the account of Pilate's wife who tried to warn her husband regarding Jesus (Matthew 27:19).

Women quickly catch on to people who use deceptive or misleading words. Women also may be more open to emotionally connect to people and help her husband to do the same.

When a wife feels free to share her insights with her husband, he can be greatly blessed by simply listening to her radar findings. Many times Rita will say, "I don't know why exactly, but I feel…" this or that. I listen. I have learned that those feelings are rarely wrong. Through the years, Rita has helped me to be aware of details I missed, feelings on which I didn't pick up, people who had hidden agendas or motives, etc.

I have written letters, made phone calls, said something, not said something, and followed a course of action many times because of Rita's radar. I thank God that He impressed me from the beginning of our marriage to listen to my wife. In an article for Rueters, John Gottman, a psychologist at the University of Washington, reported that his team followed 130 newlyweds for six years. They found that the marriages that seemed to work had one thing in common – the husband was willing to be influenced by his wife. Husbands who were not threatened by but who welcomed their wife's help in decision making had the most happy, stable marriages. The most fun part of marriage can be accepting more and more the blessings our differences can be to one another. Wives share your intuitive thoughts and encourage your husband to receive your radar as a gift for both of you.

In II Kings 4:9-10, a woman "perceived" that the prophet Elisha was a holy man and convinced her husband to help her show kindness to him. What miracle resulted because of her actions? (II Kings 4:32-37)

_____

_____

Why is it difficult for men to follow their wives' intuitive direction? How would a man's logic hinder him from heeding his wife's feelings or perceptions?

_____

_____

Husbands, are you able to recall an incident when your wife tried to warn you or inform you about her strong feelings regarding a certain individual or situation, and later she was proven correct?

_____

_____

*I Love You, You're Perfect, Now Change!*

—BROADWAY MUSICAL BY JOE DIPIETRO

Luke 9:47 is a verse that recounts an event when Jesus discerned the "thoughts of their hearts." Is it possible that a Christian wife's intuition could be a spiritual gift? How? (Read Matthew 22:18 and Hebrews 4:12 before answering.)

_____

_____

Husband, affirm your wife's gift of intuition by expressing your willingness to consider her insights before making major decisions. Assure her that her feelings and thoughts are important to you and can be beneficial to you and the family as a whole.

# CHAPTER 4

# SUCCESSFUL FAMILIES FOLLOW THE LEADERSHIP OF THE HEAD OF THE HOME

*The husband is the head…as Christ is the head of the church…and he is the Saviour.*
—*Ephesians 5:23*

Dance. When you want to avoid discussing an issue directly, that is what you do, dance around it. This important subject, the leadership of the home, is one issue many people avoid these days, dancing around it for various reasons. We will be quite direct. No dancing here.

Simply put, God intended the head of the home to be a good, loving, godly dad, husband, and father, and He says it in no uncertain terms.

Families desperately need men who will be honorable and trustworthy with the role God has given them. Ezekiel 22:30 declares, *"I looked for a man among them who would build up the wall and stand before me in the gap on behalf of the land so I would not have to destroy it, but I found none"* (NIV). What a tragic epitaph. But it is one that is still relevant today. Where are the men who will lead and stand in the gap for their wives and children? Are men going to becaome the men God called them to be? There is no greater joy or opportunity on the face of the earth.

One of my (Richard's) favorite movies is *To Kill A Mockingbird*. An attorney named Atticus Finch defends a young black man, Tom Robinson, who is accused of a crime. Throughout the trial, Atticus demonstrates tremendous dignity, character, insight, and leadership as he battles the prejudice of an already biased jury.

It is not the responsibility of the head of the home to see that everyone does what he says they are to do. It is the responsability of the head of the home to see that the family does what God says they are to do.

*Only those who struggle to learn to lead should be allowed to lead.*
—*ARISTOTLE*

On the final day of the trial, the crowd of family members and friends are gathered in the courtroom balcony. Atticus' young daughter, Scout, is seated with them. When the trial is over, the courtroom empties leaving only Atticus seated at the table gathering his things. As he stands to leave, the crowd in the gallery, which has remained behind in his honor, slowly begins to stand, one by one, until all are on their feet in honored silence. Scout, Atticus' daughter, is puzzled by the display. As Atticus strides slowly down the aisle to leave the courtroom, an old gentleman in the balcony who is standing next to the still-seated Scout leans down and says quietly to her, "Stand up girl, stand up, your daddy's passin' by!"

> **A family needs a coach, not a critic.**

Whether you're a dad or a single mom – whatever has caused your to be the head of your home – what a testimony that statement would be about your leadership!

Read I Kings 9:4 and II Chronicles 26:4. List the key leadership principles found in those verses.

_____

_____

_____

_____

_____

In the following pages, we will examine the role of the man as the "servant-leader" and the concept of submission, as taught in Scripture, as it applies to every member of the family.

When Scripture directs a husband to love his wife as Christ loved the Church, God is assigning him the responsibility to provide for, to protect, and to lead his family. Like Christ, he is to be the servant-leader of his home. The concepts of a husband's servant leadership and his family's gracious submission come from the two Greek words: *kephale* and *hupotasso*.

## KEPHALE

The word *kephale* has been translated "head" in almost all versions of the Bible. According to the *Greek-English Lexicon* by Bauer, Arndt, Danker, and Gingrich, *kephale* means "in the case of living beings, to denote a superior source of leadership...of the husband in relationship to his wife (I Corinthians 11:3,

Ephesians 5:32), and of Christ in relationship to the church as expressed in Ephesians 4:15 and 5:23."[2]

The word refers to one in "authority over." So the word *kephale* means "leader, ruler, or source." Applying their definition of the word *kephale* as "source" to I Corinthians 11:3, it reads, *"Now I want you to realize that the source of every man is Christ, and the source of the woman is man, and the source of Christ is God."* What a great compliment to you as the head of your home, whether you are a dad, a single mom, or a caregiver. To have your family say, "You are my source because I know that Christ is your source," is powerful!

Ask each member of your family what they believe their needs to be. Do their expressed needs differ from what you considered their needs to be? For each, list the need(s) below and how you, as head of the home, can be a source to meet that need.

_____

_____

_____

_____

_____

_____

*How can I possibly lead others when I have no full power and command of myself?*

—FRANCOIS RABELAIS, 1532

## HUPOTASSO

The *Greek-English Lexicon* defines the word *hupotasso* in Ephesians 5:21 as "submission in the sense of voluntarily yielding in love." It carries with it the concept "to line up under."[3] Because of the tense of the grammar, *hupotasso* refers to an activity that is ongoing and continuous; and because the word is in the middle voice, it means the action is voluntary – "to submit oneself." Thus, the wife and children are instructed to continuously, graciously, and voluntarily line up under the authority and leadership of the head of the home. Peter calls upon the head of the home, who has this incredibly important role and God-given power to be "considerate" and "treat [family members] with respect" (I Peter 3:7). Colossians 4:18 states an important principle of leadership when it admonishes, *"Husbands do not be harsh with your wives."*

The world doesn't need more macho men. It needs more Godly men.

*Men should be what they seem.*

—SHAKESPEARE, OTHELLO

Some say the concept of submission implies inferiority on the part of the individual who must submit. But Scripture clearly indicates in Ephesians 22:33 that although the husband is in the position of authority and the wife is to submit to him, they are of equal worth and equally bear God's image although they have different and distinct roles. The picture this scripture gives is of a man treating his wife in such a way that those observing his treatment of her see that he values her more than he values himself. What woman wouldn't feel comfortable being submissive to such a man?

Read Ephesians 5:25-33. What does it say a man's position should be in relationship to his attitude toward his wife? List each below.

_____

_____

_____


Now read Philippians 6:4. The head of the home is instructed to avoid a particular behavior with children. Write it here.

_____

_____


*Strike the father if you hear the son swear.*

—ROBERT BURTON, 1651

What behavior does this verse instruct you to adopt?

_____

_____


A wife is to submit herself graciously to the servant-leadership of her husband just as the church willingly submits to the headship of Christ. It is the responsibility of the head of the home to see that his wife is presented to the family in this fashion of respect and honor. He demonstrates it, for example, by standing when she comes to the table or by opening her car door. In these ways a man demonstrates that the woman is valued and respected. Don't walk ten paces ahead of your wife as if she were a possession or a "tag-along."

The key element here is to remember that the model for the head of the home is Christ Himself.

When our children were small, one of the greatest moments of my day was when I arrived home from the office. I walked in the front door to the chants of "Daddy, Daddy, Daddy! Momma, Daddy's home!"

My father was an abusive alcoholic. I remember fearing his arrival home every day until his death in an automobile accident. When I heard his car pull into the driveway, I was inmediately out the back door and on my bike to pedal as far away and as fast as I could.

As the head of your home, you can decide to lead your family by the power of love, trust, and respect, or lead as my father did – out of fear, terror, and revenge.

## AS HEAD OF THE HOME, YOU SHOULD ASK YOURSELF AND YOUR FAMILY A KEY QUESTION.

As head of our home, I realized when the children were very young that one important question should be part of my daily conversation with my children and with Rita. When I put the children to bed, before we prayed and gave each other a goodnight kiss, I always asked them this simple question:

# "DO YOU FEEL SAFE?"

This simple question could evoke conversations that would last an hour, or a simple, "Yes, Daddy, I feel safe. Good night!"

Even burly, tough-as-nails guys would relish hearing those words from their dads. What a wonderful blessing it is to your family to know that you would do anything to make sure they are safe. I still ask my children this question today, even though they're adults with careers and children of their own.

If your family isn't feeling safe, it's your responsibility as the head of the home to make it happen.

According to Isaiah 40:11, Christ cares for His own, and they feel safe in His care. The head of the home emulates this behavior to assure his family feels safe. List these characteristics here.

_____

_____

_____

_____

*How can you recognize a leader? It is easy. Is anyone following?*
—FRED SMITH

## WHEN THERE IS NO MALE LEADERSHIP.

The only person who has the right to lead is a person who knows how to be led.

Many families don't have a dad as the head of their home. If you are a single mom, grandparent, or other caregiver and are now the head of the home, you must accept that role. Your family is depending on you. Read on with an understanding that these principles apply to you just as much as they apply to a father as the head of the home.

# KEY PRINCIPLES PRACTICED DAILY BY THE HEAD OF THE HOME

**1. As the head of the home, it is your responsibility to see that your family does what God says they are to do.** Your responsibility is not to see that your family does what you say they are to do.

Deuteronomy 6:7 states the responsibilities of the head of the home regarding the above statement. List those five responsibilities here.

*One father is more good than a hundred schoolmasters.*
—*GEORGE HERBERT, 1633*

_____

_____

_____

_____

_____

**2. It is your responsibility as head of your home to lead.** The only way you can know if you're leading is simple. Is anyone following? As Norman Schwarzkoff once remarked, "If you are in command, then lead."

Deuteronomy 4:9, 31:13, and Proverb 22:6 list the characteristics of leadership needed by your family. Write them below.

_____

_____

_____

_____

_____

_____

**3. As head of your home, you should be three things to your family:**

• PROTECTOR
      1. Physically - I Timothy 3:4
      2. Emotionally - II Samuel 12:16
      3. Spiritually - I Samuel 3:13

• PROVIDER
      1. Of Stability - Ephesians 6:4; Psalm 112:2
      2. Of Physical Needs - II Corinthians 12:14
      3. Of Independence - Proverb 22:6; II Chronicles 26:4

• PRIEST
      1. Practicing Prayer - Deuteronomy 6:7
      2. Obeying God's Word - Psalm 22:4
      3. Demonstrating Obedience to God - James 1:14-15
      4. Demonstrating Consistency - Deuteronomy 4:9

**4. As head of your home, you should practice six things each day in relationship with your family:**

• *Give them unconditional love.* First John 4:12 declares that this kind of love is only possible when God dwells and rules in our heart. Read I Corinthians 13 for the characteristics of unconditional love which the head of each home must practice each day.

• *Provide them an environment for growth.* In the story of the Good Father (often called the Parable of the Prodigal Son) found in Luke 15, we see the good father provide this element for growth by providing his son with the help, guidance, fairness, and encouragement necessary for personal growth. Notice how the son said, "I will arise and go to my father" (verse 18).

• *Practice beneficial discipline.* Proverb 6:20 tells us, *"My son, keep thy father's commandment and forsake not forsake the law of thy mother."* The word "commandment" literally means, "to teach with discipline." In contrast, the word "teaching" means instruction. Fathers are the enforcers of discipline, and mothers are the "re-enforcers." God's perfect plan is for a child to have the benefit of both parents in the home.

*He who leads is always leading from his spirit, never from his head.*
—DEMOSTHENES

*Whoever obeys truth, it is to him others listen most intently.*
—HOMER

*Practice what you preach.*

—*Titus Plautus, 128 b.c.*

• *Provide consistent and fair guidance.* First Thessalonians 2:11-12 demonstrates three ways in which you can do this. You cannot do one unless you do all three. Explain in your own words how you would demonstrate each in your family.

Exhort - to advise, urge, and earnestly caution.

_____

_____

_____

Comfort – to soothe, console, and cheer.

_____

_____

_____

To keep your family trusting you, admit when you're wrong and keep quiet about it when you are right.

Charge – to lay upon a command, instruction, and accountability for action.

_____

_____

_____

• *Exhibit merciful forgiveness.* See the example of the good father in Luke 15:19-20.

• *Revere the members of the family and strive to meet their needs.* See Matthew 7:9-12.

If you want your family to grow to love and honor God, then, as the head of the home, show them what a person looks like who loves and honors God. There is no substitute for that kind of example. Be that example of God's love every day.

# CHAPTER 5

# SUCCESSFUL FAMILIES MEET THE NEEDS OF THEIR CHILDREN

*Children are an heritage of the LORD.*
—*Psalm 127:3*

Do you ever think your children belong to you? They don't. They're gifts that God *entrusted* to you. You are responsible to see they become all that God intended them to be.

God wants men and women to make moral decisions. He placed you, the parent, in your role as the guide, teacher, counselor, and model of that kind of mature behavior. Because you cannot always be at your child's side helping with all of their decisions, you must help them develop the necessary skills to make decisions when you are not there – decisions that will be sound and of good judgment. The voice of moral, sensible leadership needs to eventually come from within them and not from you.

In a recent *Dennis the Menace* cartoon, Dennis is standing in the corner after getting in trouble again. Red-faced, he shouts, "If you're raising me the right way, then how come I get in so much trouble?" Dennis' words hit home for many of us who have become extremely frustrated with our role as parents.

The principles in this chapter must be used to develop a godly system which will produce His desired result for your children, as you exercise your best skill with this "art form." We are going to try, in the following pages, to help you find out what motivates your children so you may use those parenting techniques, and also what demoralizes them so that you may avoid those.

When considering how to meet the needs of our children, we must realize one thing. There are no perfect parents. Even the most diligent parent has some

*What is more important than to take a human being and create in that person what they are capable of becoming?*

—*PROFESSOR HENRY HIGGINS, MY FAIR LADY*

Prepare your children for the time when they have the right to do what they think is right to do.

*I would that my father and my mother had minded about who and what they were before they begot me.*

—*LAURENCE STERN, 1760*

regret about a time they wish they had done something differently with their child, or a decision they wish they could retract. In reality, God asked us as parents to obey the Word, follow the example of Christ, and simply do our best.

Parenting is more of an art than science. We joke about this in our workshops, but in reality when we say parenting is an art, we mean it. Science gives us predictable and unchanging laws and principles. But in parenting, we're painting on a canvas that is the life of the child. It takes different brush strokes and variations in color to make the painting come to life.

Parenting is a very demanding occupation. Every parent has a laundry list of their own of successes, near misses, and failures. Early in our marriage, we made an important choice that helped us immensely. We decided that if we were going to become parents, we would make it our full-time job. We, like many parents, had to do a lot of "on-the-job-training," and we didn't get an "operations manual" at the hospital. Parenting demanded skills we didn't have but needed to learn quickly.

Sir Roy Calne, a leading British doctor from Cambridge University, has suggested that people should be required to pass a parenting test and gain a "reproduction license" before being allowed to have children. He proposed a law that would establish a minimum age of 25 before anyone would be allowed to have a child. "Everyone endorses the idea of a driving license or hunting license as recognition you have certain skills," he said. "Bringing a child into the world is far more important, and I put forward the licensing of this activity as a serious suggestion for consideration."[4]

*Kids, I don't know what's wrong with these kids today.*
—"BYE BYE BIRDIE"
BY LEE ADAMS

This is indeed a strong suggestion, but it does have some merit for consideration, especially since young people who are barely out of puberty have made sexual choices which have thrust them into the world of parenthood long before they are emotionally ready. Being a parent is not for the faint of heart, and it's certainly not for adolescents who are mere children themselves.

Before we examine the needs of children, we want to establish some initial guidelines for parents.

### • A PARENT'S FIRST PRIORITY IS FOR THEIR CHILDREN TO HEAR THE GOSPEL AND HAVE THE OPPORTUNITY TO COME TO KNOW CHRIST.

As a parent, you should be the first to tell the Gospel to your children. You shouldn't pass this responsibility on to anyone else. It's not only your mandate, but it is also your privilege to live the principles which changed your life, as a testimony to your children. You should pray with and for your children. Pray for their salvation and make every opportunity for this most important life-changing experience to take place.

Children will be drawn to those things that are important to their parents. A recent survey conducted by the National Institute for Family Issues in Washington, D.C. provided some very interesting information. It revealed that if the mother and the father both attend church regularly, 72 percent of their children would be faithful church attendees as adults. If only dad attends regularly, 55 percent will remain faithful. If only mom attends regularly, only 15 percent remain faithful.[5]

Help your children learn the discipline of what they have to do until they can do what they were meant to do.

## If neither parent attends church regularly, only 6 percent of their children will attend as adults.

Read III John 4. What does it say is the greatest joy a parent can have?

_____

### • CHILDREN NEED BOTH PARENTS IN THE HOME.

The concept of the nuclear family is under attack today. God's perfect plan is a two-parent home in which both a mother and a father are guiding the children. God knew exactly what He was doing. The mother and father have different roles, attitudes, skills, and priorities in the child's life and upbringing.

A husband and wife must find a healthy way to be the best parents they can be. Good parents are fulfilled and whole themselves. They have a sense of well-being in their work, love, friendship, and community. Children need role models to teach them kindness toward others and responsibility for themselves. They need to feel warmth, stability, love, and a sense of safety.

Even in a single-parent home children can acquire stable family values. If you are rearing children by yourself, you are actually not alone. In answer to your prayers, God will fill the void and meet the needs of your children.

Read Job 29:12, Psalm 68:5, and Hosea 14:3. What promises are made to children who are missing a parent(s)?

_____

_____

### • CHILDREN SHOULD BE *REARED*, NOT *RAISED*!

You "raise" cattle and corn, not children. Cattle and corn only need time, food and water to survive. Children need considerably more. You "rear" your children in the nurture and admonition of the Lord. To rear a child is to take great interest in the child's emotional, spiritual, and educational growth. You are much more interested in what the child will become than in simply seeing the child grow physically. To raise a child is to let the child set their own course, make their own decisions, and step toward adulthood in their own devices and abilities.

Read I Timothy 4:6 and explain how a child is to be nourished.

_____

_____

### • EACH CHILD IS UNIQUE.

*Dear Poppa, Thank you for taking me out on a date. You love me like you love mommy and I like that a lot. Love, your princess.*

—TRINITY TATE

Each member of your family is as unique, different, and beautiful in their own way as a snowflake is. Anyone who has more than one child knows about differences in learning styles and behavior. Some children can be disciplined with a stern look; others fail to respond to the sternest reprimands. Effective child training requires parents to customize their methods to the individual child.

Our children were so different in the way each responded that we sometimes wondered how they came from the same family!

Parents should do what Jesus did. He started with people where they were, at the level of ability and commitment they had at that moment. He always saw their potential and never left them where they were when they first came to Him. He never lowered His standards.

Always meet your children where they are, but have a plan to help them get where they need to go.

Rita and I have entered the stage in our life which has been called the "empty nest." Our children are all grown and have their own families. We joke that now we're finally ready to be parents! If you are not a parent yet, think and pray with great diligence before you make the decision to become one. If you are already a parent, consider the following principles with great diligence as you make the task of parenting one of your most important commitments.

Before you begin this section of study, answer the following question and write down your thoughts.

Are children more like wet cement, or a chalkboard?

_____
_____
_____

# THE FIVE BASIC NEEDS OF CHILDREN

## 1. CHILDREN NEED UNCONDITIONAL LOVE.

The importance of children knowing they are loved unconditionally is immeasurable. Unconditional love is the kind of love God offers to us as His children. He loves us unconditionally, not for anything we can do for Him, but for who we are – His children.

Your children need to receive that same unconditional love from you – a love that doesn't depend on performance or ability, a love that gives them security, peace, and confidence.

God speaks of His beloved Son in Matthew 3:17. It is important to note that at this time Jesus had never preached a sermon or performed one miracle. Yet God glowingly affirmed His Son. Complete the verse below.

*"A voice from heaven, saying, This is my beloved Son,* _____ _____ ___
_____ _____ _____."*

In the same manner that God affirmed His Son, you should tell your children often that you are pleased and blessed they are in your life. Your children need

*"I'm writing a book on raising children."*
*"But we don't have any children."*
*"That's why I have time to write a book."*
—"THE WIZARD OF ID,"
JUNE 28, 1992

to hear they are loved whether they succeed or fail, whether their behavior is acceptable or unacceptable. God's love and parental love should be the two certainties in your child's life.

What does Romans 8:39 tell us could separate us from the love of God?

_____

_____

## PARENTS TRYING TO RESOLVE THEIR PERSONAL PROBLEMS AND FAILURES THROUGH THEIR CHILDREN GIVE CONDITIONAL LOVE.

You can easily recognize these parents. They're trying to make up for their own failures or shortcomings by "reliving" their lives through their children. They expect their children to play a sport, join a club, or perform in a particular way, all the time pressuring the child to "do it for me."

Parents who attempt to resolve past personal issues through their children are often unaware of the psychological damage they are inflicting. When you pressure a child to do something that the child is not gifted to do, you have programmed that child to fail. Not only will the child feel humiliation and a lack of confidence, the child will develop a tremendous sense of guilt because he has failed his parent(s).

After this occurs two or three times the child will simply give up and not try anything at all because of the fear of failure. Even talented children who do well in sports, music, or the classroom must be motivated by seeing the benefit for themselves personally – not for someone else. Some parents feel a sense of worth and success only through the achievements of their children. Often a child is pressured to keep the family happy by continuing to perform. Should the child fail, that failure sends the entire family into a tailspin because the family's success was measured by the child's success. What an overwhelming burden for any child to carry.

Parents should encourage children to try different sports, studies, and creative pursuits, but only to discover the child's natural interest and gifts. Those parents who want their children to make up for whatever shortcomings they had themselves must relieve the child from that kind of responsibility. Sometimes

*I won't let you down, your face will not frown. The time is near, even this year! So let me go, without a fear, and as I leave, we'll cry a unified tear.*

—RYAN TATE

parents were successful at something as children, and they expect their children to continue those pursuits even when they are not equipped, or are not capable, or have no desire to do so. Remember, parents, your child is not you! It's a wonderful adventure to celebrate the uniqueness of your child and discover together what they are gifted to do.

Four things will kill a child's spirit:
1. Always feeling they're bad
2. Always feeling they're in trouble
3. Always feeling inadequate and that they don't live up to expectations
4. Always hearing their parents compare them to other children

List some of the ways you love your children unconditionally that have nothing to do with their performance or ability. Consider sharing them with your child.

_____

_____

_____

In a television interview after she had received the Nobel Peace Prize, Mother Teresa was asked: "What can the average person do to promote world peace?" Her wise counsel was this: "If you want to promote world peace, go home and love your family."

## 2. CHILDREN NEED TO BE TRAINED.

> *Train up a child in the way he should go: and when he is old, he will not depart from it.*
> —Proverb 22:6

Proverb 22:6 contains a key element here. It states we are to "train up" a child. The concept behind the Hebrew term translated "train up" is derived from the palate or roof of the mouth. Specifically, it was used to describe a rope placed in the mouth of a horse to give it direction. It was also used to describe the action of a midwife who, shortly after the birth of a child, dipped her finger in a tiny pool of crushed grapes or dates and then massaged the baby's gums to stimulate sucking. Thus, the phrase "train up" carried the idea of cultivating a thirst within a child to know and learn.

*Virtue is harder to be got than a knowledge of the word; and, if lost in a young man, is seldom recovered.*
— *JOHN LOCKE*

The verse does not command a parent to "teach" a child. To teach is to simply pass on information with a possible test at the end. There is not the personal involvement or commitment in teaching that there is in training. When you train, you become "hands on" in the experience and effort. Training requires doing it again and again until the child gets it.

When Proverb 22:6 speaks of training up a child "in the way he should go" it literally means to observe the unique characteristics, interests, strengths, and abilities of the child as you do the training. So the Word instructs clearly that training should be unique to each child.

The verse concludes with the promise that, *"when he is old he will not depart from it."* That's a wonderful promise to every parent who may be wondering if his or her children will ever "get it!" In the original Hebrew language, the word "old" means "mature."

> You show your love best for your children by giving them what you believe they need, not what they tell you they want.

If you will continue your training with perseverance, God's Word promises that when the child "wakes up," matures, they will return to those truths you have implanted in their lives. The only condition of this promise is that you train consistently and effectively. For instance, children need instruction in morality by your example. Children don't learn morality from what you tell them, but from how you treat them. You're their bridge from innocence to maturity.

An ancient Japanese proverb makes this very clear when it admonishes parents, "Do not teach your children to be successful; teach them to be moral."

Children need parents who will model respect for authority. That includes respect for teachers, adults, and others who have positions of authority.

## PARENTS MUST REALIZE THAT WITH CHILDREN MORE IS CAUGHT THAN IS TAUGHT.

> *The only defense against the world is a thorough knowledge of it.*
> —JOHN LOCK

It is true that a child learns more by observation than by any other method. However, there are three ways parents can begin to train a child from the time the child is very young.

- First, do it *for* the child to show them how.
- Second, do it *with* the child assisting each step of the way.
- Third, allow the child to do the task *without your help*.

A child needs lessons, not advice. A child needs to know that you will listen to them. Children should be reflections, not extensions, of their parents.

## TRAIN YOUR CHILDREN BY BEING *AUTHORITATIVE* INSTEAD OF *AUTHORITARIAN*.

Children often see their parents as distant, removed, impossible to please, and demanding beyond reason or understanding. To a child, a parent demonstrates maturity more by their behavior than by their instructions – by what they do, not what they say.

The problem is, many parents don't understand that a child needs, and really wants, their instruction.

How a child receives that instruction is dependent on the way it's given. Too many parents consider themselves "the law of the land." They give their children the impression that "it's, my way or the highway." They're authoritarian – unbending, inflexible, and callous toward the child. "Just do what I say and stop asking so many questions!" barks the authoritarian parent. Eventually, the child loses all hope and stops asking and listening altogether.

The authoritative parent, however, has a wealth of information and rich personal experience which they are eager to share with their child. They allow questions, mistakes, and errors in judgment, seeing them as wonderful opportunities to teach and train their child.

Your children will seek you out if they believe you are a caring source of information who will not berate them simply because they don't know something. Teach them everything you know as one who is authoritative, not as an unyielding authoritarian. Most parents who are authoritarian in their behavior are actually fearful of not knowing what to do and are afraid to admit it. John Locke said it best: "It's one thing to show a child that he is in error; it is quite another to put him in possession of the truth."

Read Ephesians 6:1-3. What is the promise to one who obeys and honors their father and mother?

_____

What is the most motivating thing you can do for a son? Tell him you're pleased with him.

Ephesians 6:4 gives an example of an authoritarian parent. To what does this parent "provoke" a child?

_____

Hebrews 10:24 gives an example of an authoritative parent. To what does this parent "provoke" a child?

_____

Children mature faster when you give them a track to follow and on which to grow. Having a purpose reduces their frustration. Having a clear purpose has two essential parts: what we should do, and what we should not do.

Part of nurturing a child is to give them direction and loving understanding. As the parent you are the manager of your child's growth and maturation. You can train your child in self-discipline in two ways: by accountability and by setting expectations. When children know what is expected of them and are held accountable, they learn how to be independent and responsible for their own actions.

## TRAIN YOUR CHILDREN BY ALLOWING THEM TO MAKE MISTAKES

Children need to know that life can be hard. They will need to be prepared. Children must be allowed to fail, but also be expected, with your help and encouragement, to take responsibility for their actions and correct them. The struggle in overcoming difficulties strengthens and prepares children for the challenges of life.

The English biologist Alfred Russell Wallace made an observation that illustrates this very well. An emperor butterfly emerging from its chrysalis was moving about inside its prison, struggling with all its feeble might to get free. Pitying the struggling creature and thinking to help the process along, Wallace slit the chrysalis open with his knife. Did a beautiful new butterfly flit out and spread its wings in the glorious sunshine? No! On the contrary, the butterfly emerged but grew weaker and perished before his eyes. Wallace concluded that the butterfly's struggle out of the prison of the chrysalis was essential to give it the strength it needed to survive.[6]

Enzymes secreted during the struggle to escape the chrysalis create a butterfly's colorful wings. Amazingly, predators that see the beautiful colors of the butterfly's wings consider the butterfly to be poisonous. So not only does the struggle make the butterfly strong, it also creates a lifelong defense against its enemies.

The same principle applies to our children. In much the same manner as the struggles of the butterfly, the struggles of our children are essential to make them strong and capable adults. Parents who wish to train their children well, will give them guidance and help them realize that life's not always fair…in fact, life can be downright hard! But just as the butterfly's struggle is necessary for its survival, their own struggles are the necessary precursors to victory and success. Children need to be allowed to experience adversity and handle it on their own.

Adversity is keenly important in:
- Character development
- Career development
- Relationship development

Isaiah 48:10 declares that God causes us to walk through difficult times for what purpose?

_____

## 3. CHILDREN NEED TO BE NURTURED.

The word "nurture" means "to provide nourishment and support during the fragile stages of development." It is imperative that parents provide this nurture with words, with touch, and with their time.

### CHILDREN NEED TO BE TOUCHED IN ORDER TO FEEL NURTURED.
Kids need to grow up in families that hug, kiss, and let one another know they are loved. Many children never grow up seeing their parents hug on one another.

### CHILDREN ALSO NEED THEIR PARENTS' TIME.
It has been said that parents need to spend more quality time with their children. What exactly does that mean? We are of the opinion that any time you spend with your children is not wasted. It is quality time. But the quantity of time is also important to a child. Most children are aching for more time with their parents.

*He that would have his son have a respect for him and his orders must have a great reverence and respect for his son.*

—JOHN LOCKE, 1693

*Children need a lot more than just money. What they need most is love and time and attention.*

—CONGRESSMAN JOHN DUNCAN, JR.

John Maxwell conducted a survey in which he asked over 1,500 children, "What makes for happy families?" Over 90 percent gave the same answer: "Doing things together." Taking time to be with one another, that's how children recognize love.[7]

Our children wanted our time. I (Rita) will never forget a note our son Ryan left for his dad when Ryan was just a little guy. The note may have needed some work on the spelling, but the message came across loud and clear:

> I wont (want) to go fishing and go play footbol (football) and play bayseboll (baseball) and resel (wrestle). And I mit (might) wont (want) to tace (take) croty-lesens (karate lessons) but I mite (might) not. But wote (what) I wont (want) to do moste (most) is spind (spend) more time! This is for you!

I love the admonition at the end of our son's note when he wrote, "This is for you!" Richard has kept that small scrap of paper (which still hangs on his office wall) for almost twenty years as a treasured reminder of this important principle. Parents, your children want, deserve, and need your time.

Many parents of this generation believe that the time they spend with their children needs to be time spent entertaining them or spending money on them. This is not so. Your children would rather take a simple walk with you and have your undivided attention than spend an afternoon at an expensive amusement park. Children yearn to feel your approval, your touch, and your love. That takes more than a brief dash in and out of their lives.

Read James 4:14 and write the description James gives about life and its brevity.

_____

Scripture admonishes us to make time with our children a priority – above our schedules and careers. Nurture your children with your time.

## 4. CHILDREN NEED GENUINE, DESERVED PRAISE.

In addition to needing their parents' touch and time, children need to be nurtured with their parents' words.

*Authority without wisdom will bruise but will not polish.*
—ANNE BRADSTREET, 1664

Realize that there is a difference between flattery and genuine praise. Flattery is unearned. Flattery heaps compliments on a child for something he or she did not achieve. Praise, on the other hand, is used to reinforce positive, constructive behavior. It should be specific. Parents should watch for ways to offer genuine, well-deserved praise while avoiding empty flattery.

Praise a child for genuine character traits. Praise your children for who they *are* more than for what they *do*.

The current trend for building self-esteem tells a child, "You are special, no matter what!" But praise alone will not produce high achievement. According to the research published in the November 2001 issue of *Personality and Social Psychology Review,* while self-esteem among America's youth has been on the rise for the past thirty years, accomplishment and responsible decision making have been on the decline.[5] Why? Because the bloated self-esteem of many of America's children is not based on a realistic appraisal of their strengths and weaknesses, which leads to accomplishment. Rather, it is based on an unconditional, uncritical acceptance of whatever they do and think, which leads to mediocrity. It's not praise. It's flattery.[8]

High expectations coupled with accurate, supportive feedback produce high achievement, which merits praise. Effort is certainly worthy of your praise. Children have become addicted not to achievement, which is a result of hard work and effort, but to entitlement. They may continue to expect the same treatment from spouses, employers, and the world system as they grow older.

*I love you dearly, Mom, and miss you. Most of all I miss your touch.*

—RYAN TATE

What do you believe to be the difference between flattery and praise?

_____

_____

Read Proverbs 26:28 in *The Living Bible*. What does this verse say flattery is really a form of and why?

_____

_____

Continuing in that same verse, how does the word "hatred" impact your understanding of the truth in this verse? What does "flattery" mean about the person doing the flattering?

_____

_____

**YOU CAN PRAISE YOUR CHILDREN IN FOUR WAYS:**

1. PRAISE SELECTIVELY

   Praise behavior that reflects your desires and goals for your children. Indiscriminate praise doesn't motivate; it only confuses. It is a myth that children learn obedience by flattery.

2. PRAISE IMMEDIATELY

   Catch your children in the act of doing a good deed and praise them at that time. Delayed praise has less meaning than immediate praise.

3. PRAISE SPECIFICALLY

   Use specifics as, "I love the way you shared your toy with your sister," or "What a good job you did making your bed today!"

4. PRAISE INTENTIONALLY

   Look for ways to praise a child with a goal in mind. When you want your children to learn to be kind, praise acts of kindness. Expect your children to be kind and tell them you are not at all surprised at their kind behavior.

You can nurture your children with your words by admitting your mistakes. Children need parents who will admit their faults and weaknesses and say, "I'm sorry." We sometimes say stupid things to our children and then wonder why they don't listen to us. You must be fair. Correct things in yourself before you try to correct things in your child.

Use these five questions and statements regularly with your children. You'll revolutionize your relationship with your children if they hear these words often:

- "I am proud of the choice you just made."
- "What do you think about…?"
- "Would you like to have my opinion about that?"
- "Here are several options I think you should consider. Whatever you decide, I will stand with you."
- "Since we cannot find a way to say 'yes,' here is why we have to say 'no'."

## 5. Children Need Parents Who Are in Control.

Is your child out of control? Before we begin our discussion of this important subject, examine the list below. Do any of these statements apply to you?

- You let your child have their way just to stop their complaining.
- You let your child interrupt you.
- You hate to disappoint your child.
- You can't stand to see your child cry.
- You ignore misbehavior.
- You make empty threats.
- You "ask" your child to obey instead of expecting the child to obey.

### Teach Them Obedience

Karl Menninger once said, "What is done to children, they will do to society."[9] Too many children have been taught to be self-centered and demanding by parents who were poor examples. Some children have had no role models at all and, consequently, society suffers from their lack of discipline and character. Children need limits which are expressed in boundaries and control.

Controlling your children means that you require obedience. You must teach your child the benefits of self-control. If you are a parent with no boundaries or expectations, your children will become self-centered and demanding.

## CHILDREN DO NOT ALWAYS NEED TO UNDERSTAND IN ORDER TO OBEY.

According to Scripture, God is more pleased with obedience than with sacrifice. This is a good rule for parents to follow as well.

Children don't recognize danger when they're young. You must teach them to trust your judgment and authority. An old proverb states this concept very well: "A child does not fear the hungry lion." As a parent, you have encountered that lion many times and must protect your child by expecting obedience. Teach your child that their actions and choices have consequences.

When you tell your child not to ride their bike in the street, they don't understand why you, as a parent, would refuse their fun. The street's bigger, wider, and smoother than the sidewalk. They don't understand the dangers involved. In fact, they might complain all day about not being allowed to ride

God says "no" once in order to be able to say, "yes" twice. Yes to protection from the consequences of the action and yes to provision, a better way to live with greater blessing.

in the street. But as a loving parent, you still expect them to obey, because their safety depends on it.

We would have loved it if our children had been delighted when we asked them to make their beds or clean up their toys. That never seemed to happen. But we expected obedience anyway, and they learned a valuable lesson.

In his senior year at college, our son Ryan astonished us when he said that what he was most grateful for was the fact that we had set boundaries and expected obedience from him when he was growing up. But you wouldn't have known it when he was in junior high school.

You can teach your children about your love for them with your skilled control of them.

In I Timothy 3:4, how does Scripture describe parents who are in control of their children?

_____

It's hard work to be diligent. Many people do not think the disobedience of children is serious. Read Romans 1:30 and II Timothy 3:2 to discover how serious God believes disobedience of children to be.

_____

_____

_____

*Parenting a child involves knowing that each child goes through a series of stages and a parent must change as each stage comes along.*

*—DARRYL OWENS*

## KNOW HOW AND WHEN TO SAY "NO."

Some parents fear denying their children anything, and their children are usually emotionally out-of-control, attention-hungry, and extremely selfish. Parents should learn that saying "no" will not kill a child; it won't even make them sick!

When a parent loves a child, saying no is often the most loving, caring thing to do. For the child's benefit there are things that he must not be allowed to say, do, or be. Will the child like it? No. Will you be the child's best friend? No. But you will have taken a more important role as parent.

On the other hand, some parents say no too often. The child's every request is met with a quick no. How demoralizing to a child to realize that they will always get the same answer! That there are no discussions, no options, no alternatives – just the word no. This parental attitude can be as devastating as never saying no to a child.

In observing parents who said no too quickly, we saw how the practice deflated the child. The practice dashed the child's tiniest hope. So when our children were small, we determined that we wanted them to feel that their every request, no matter how small, was important and was one that would be considered thoughtfully. Instead of just saying the quick and final no to their request, we began to say to them,

## "LET'S SEE IF THERE'S A WAY WE CAN SAY 'YES' TO THAT."

When they knew that Mom and Dad would seriously consider the request, there was optimism that we would be fair and consider their thoughts and feelings on the matter. Many times, as we examined the request in detail the children themselves would conclude, "I shouldn't do this right now," or, "I don't really need that thing," or, "I will think about this some more." It was a great parenting tool.

*He who does not punish evil commands it to be done.*
—LEONARDO DA VINCI

A father in California emailed us his experience regarding this principle after he heard us discuss it in one of our seminars:

"I was always so quick to say 'no' to my son and really didn't think about what I was doing. After hearing your concept, I decided to give it a try. The very next day my son came flying up the driveway on his bicycle with a request. 'Dad, Jimmy and his family are going to Disneyland for the weekend. Can I go with them?' I almost blurted out my usual 'no,' but caught myself in the nick of time and said, 'Well, let's see if we can find a way to say yes to that.' The surprised look on his face was priceless. I thought he was going to fall off his bike. He was unaccustomed to such treatment by his dad. We sat down on the porch and talked about money for the trip, events his mom had planned for the weekend, and several other issues. After a few minutes of this kind of conversation, my son decided, 'Dad, I think I'll just stay home. Thanks for thinking about it with me.' He was back on his bike in a flash and was nothing but a blur as he headed down the street to play. That event occurred about a month ago. Now he comes to me with almost every request and starts by saying, 'Dad, do you think there is a way we could say yes to…' Our relationship has never been better, and he has become more responsible. I thank you for this idea; it really does work."

If you say "no" too often to a child, the child will become defeated, frustrated, and bitter. If you never say "no" to a child, the child will become a victim of too much freedom and self-indulgence.

Proverb 19:18 encourages parents to take what action with a child before it is too late?

_____

According to Proverbs 3:11-12, what is the most loving thing a parent can do for his child?

_____

# BE CONSISTENT AND FAIR WITH DISCIPLINE.

There is a tremendous difference betweeen discipline and punishment. Punishment has at its very core an intention to bring harm, fear, pain, and distress. Its purpose is not to teach or train. It results in fear and overpowering anger. Discipline, however, brings learning, benefit, and positive growth. There is no harm intended, only nurture. Proverb 29:17 says it well: *Correct thy son, and he shall give thee rest; yea, he shall give delight unto they soul.*

Administer discipline for acts of disobedience. Don't discipline your child in anger or haste. Discipline your child in private. Never tell your child that they're bad. What they did might have been bad, but they themselves are not. Have your child repeat to you why they are being disciplined. Discipline is important because it gives the child the knowledge that a price has been paid. Take as much time to love on your child as you did to administer the discipline. Do not remind the child again of what they did wrong.

*Only a fully-engaged parent offers discipline and a high expectation of achievement coupled with complete support.*

—*RICHARD LOUVE*

What does I Thessalonians 2:11 say are the three ways parents provide their children the tools needed to reach maturity?

1. We are to _____, which means to advise and caution.
2. We are to _____, which means to soothe, console, and cheer up.
3. We are to_____, which means to sometimes

get tough and lay a command upon them in clear instruction, which expects obedience.

Carefully watch what you say, because *if you say it, you must do it.* Many parents yell and threaten their children, but never follow through with the proper discipline, and therefore their children get their own way. A disciplined child will bring great delight to parents, while the child left alone will bring shame to the home. Don't threaten them with a punishment you don't intend to carry out. Bite your tongue rather than utter a threat on which you don't intend to follow through. If you threaten to get rid of the toys if they are not picked up, then the toys must disappear. If you don't follow through, you will send the message that you don't mean what you say, and your child will learn to ignore you.

## SPARE THE ROD AND SPOIL THE CHILD?

Before you continue, read Proverb 13:24. What does this verse say is the only proper godly motivation for the discipline of a child?

_____

_____

In your own words, write the reason(s) you think discipline is such a controversial issue.

_____

_____

_____

Before you continue a study of God's philosophy about disciplining children, write your current philosophy of discipline.

_____

_____

_____

_____

Read Proverbs 13:24 in *The Amplified Bible.* How can two words like "love," and "hate" be used in the same verse about a child? What does the verse mean by "early?"

_____

_____

*Dad, I love you.*

—*DAVID TATE IN A NOTE HE LEFT ON THE WINDSHIELD BEFORE PLAYING IN A HIGH SCHOOL FOOTBALL GAME*

Proverb 13:24 offers a great deal of practical wisdom regarding corporal punishment and the discipline of children. Unruly and spoiled children are not the blessings that the Bible says they should be to their parents. Without boundaries, children will feel lost. Discipline should only be administered for direct disobedience. Ask your child only once to obey. If they don't, sit down with them and ask if they understand why you are concerned. Ask them if they understand that discipline is necessary.

## WHAT IS THE PROPER WAY TO DISCIPLINE A CHILD?

There has been much debate on the subject of corporal punishment or the spanking of a child. Corporal punishment simply means bodily punishment, while various dictionaries define spanking as: to strike with something flat, as the open hand, especially on the buttocks.

This is what the Bible says about spanking:

Proverbs 22:15: *Foolishness is bound in the heart of a child; but the rod of correction shall drive it far from him.*

Proverbs 23:13-14: *Withhold not correction from the child: for if thou beatest him with the rod, he shall not die. Thou shalt beat him with the rod, and shalt deliver his soul from hell.*

## THE PURPOSE OF SPANKING IS NOT TO BRING PHYSICAL HARM, BUT SPIRITUAL WHOLENESS.

The discipline of children should begin at an early age, when children first begin to disobey their parents. Notice the Bible says that all children have foolishness in their hearts. The biblical definition of a fool means one who is a rebel. All children have rebellion in them; when it surfaces, it is our duty as parents to drive it out of them. You have to "crack the shell" without damaging the "nut" inside.

We are to do this by disciplining them on their "backside" with an appropriate instrument that *is in our hand but is not our hand.*

Your hand is meant for loving and encouraging. Your child should not fear your hands. Do not use your hands, but aslo never use anything that would cause permanent physical damage. A spanking should be swift and shortlived with just enough pain to make its point. We would instruct our children to get the "instrument," which was a small belt in Dad's closet. They were never afraid of our approach with our hand, but they did understand the instrument. There is an old saying that certainly applies here: "You put the board of education to the seat of understanding!" We would ask our child what they thought was a reasonable disciplinary action to help them remember this lesson. Dad, not Mom, would send them to their room to lie on the bed and think about their actions. We would tell them, "We love you, but we don't like what you did." After they had had time to think for a few minutes, we would go to their room. Richard would say to them, "Here comes the swat. Are you ready?" They were usually already close to tears being shed. The swat, or swats if necessary, were hardly enough to cause a breeze, but you would have thought they were much worse by the volume of tears. *After* the discipline was over, we would spend an equal amount of time in loving on our child.

## THE SMALL PAIN A CHILD FEELS NOW FROM A SPANKING IS TO PREVENT THEM FROM EXPERIENCING TREMENDOUS PAIN LATER IF THEY DO NOT LEARN DISCIPLINE.

Is spanking child abuse? Are you teaching your child to hit by hitting them? Some would say a child should never be disciplined in this way.

In 1998 the *Kansas City Star* conducted a survey of inmates in Leavenworth prison. Seventy-eight percent said they were never spanked as a child.

They said they had been abused and often beaten within an inch of their lives. Some said they thought their parent was going to kill them through their "discipline," but they were never spanked in the way the Word of God teaches.

The problem is that many parents, who are out of control themselves, abuse their children by beating them in an angry rage. *This* is child abuse. Parents who do this are sick and in need of help themselves. If you or your spouse are abusing your children, you can get help *now*. Call the National Child Abuse Helpline at 1-800-555-1212. It's a confidential call, and there is help if you are "at the end of your rope." You must not allow a child to suffer in this way. As a victim of child abuse myself, I (Richard) know that it can take years of help and a miracle from God to find healing and wholeness as an adult who was abused as a child.

*Autocratic and demanding parents use controlling behavior to hide their own feelings of inadequacy and failure.*

*—CONNIE SCHULTZ*

# SPANKING IS NOT CHILD ABUSE. WHEN DONE IN THE RIGHT WAY, BY THE RIGHT PERSON, WITH THE RIGHT MOTIVE AND THE RIGHT GOAL, IT DOES NOT TEACH A CHILD TO HIT.

Proverb 19:18 instructs us: *Discipline your son while there is hope, but do not (indulge your angry resentments by undue chastisements and) set yourself to his ruin* (AMP).

Read Proverbs 29:15, 17 in *The Amplified Bible*. Parents want to be proud of their children and not to worry about them. What do these verses say will create those two results?

_____

_____

_____

## BE "PARENT-ORIENTED," NOT "CHILD-ORIENTED."

*It is the time you have wasted on your rose that makes the rose so important.*

—THE FOX, THE LITTLE PRINCE.

The successful parent must be parent-oriented for the wellbeing of the child. Too many parents become consumed with meeting their child's every wish. Of course, parents should provide care, protection, and love for a child, but when the family's interests revolve around how a child feels or thinks, or what a child does or doesn't want to do, the family is child-oriented. This negative situation can lead a child to become selfish, demanding, and manipulative. Your family unit is not a cruise ship, and you're not the ship's recreational director. You're the captain.

## THE MOST IMPORTANT THING A MAN CAN DO FOR HIS CHILDREN IS TO LOVE AND CHERISH THEIR MOTHER!

Husband, remember that you married your wife because you wanted her, not because you saw an opportunity to have children.

In a child-oriented family, the marriage relationship can take second place to the overwhelming need of one or both parents to be liked by their child. The child-oriented parent wants to be their child's best friend. They must realize before it is too late that a child needs them to be their parents, not their friends. Usually, one cannot be both.

The following is a table that includes ways to identify whether or not your family is child-oriented or parent-oriented:

*Time is the most valuable thing a person can spend.*

—THEOPHRASTUS, 278 B.C.

| CHILD-ORIENTED | PARENT-ORIENTED |
|---|---|
| One parent sides with the child against the other parent in family disputes. | Parents present a united front and agree in family disputes. |
| Child's behavior is often excused. There is little discipline. | Child's behavior is quickly disciplined with punishment that fits the infraction. |
| Child is "threatened" with discipline, but there is little follow through. Rules are fuzzy. | Child is made to know and understand rules of behavior and is disciplined for willful disobedience. Rules are clear and consistent. |
| Child is rescued time and again from situations that he has caused instead of being allowed to face or deal with consequences of his own actions. | Parents know the importance of a child learning from mistakes. They support fair discipline from teachers, law-enforcement officers, and other authorities who attempt to discipline the child. |
| Child pits one parent against the other for his/her own benefit. | Child knows that parents will not be played against one another. |
| Child controls the emotional climate of the family. Family activities or plans revolve around how the child behaves or feels at any given time. Child may be too forceful and gets angry easily, even at play. | Parents do not allow the child to dictate the plans of the family by his poor behavior or attitude. The child knows the parents will not be manipulated by his outbursts of anger or periods of pouting. |
| Child blames parents and others when he has done something wrong. Child can be abusive physically or verbally and threatens parents or others with harm. | Parent will not allow the child to make them responsible for his poor behavior. Parent will never tolerate fits of rage or physical displays of violence or anger. |

Children need the control and boundaries set by loving parents. Even a teenager who tries to test those boundaries will someday understand their importance. Children who have the ability to make good choices in life will benefit immensely from the lessons learned from self-control.

As your children demonstrate their trustworthiness by obedience, you will be able to allow them more latitude and liberty.

## CHILDREN NEED PARENTS WHO KNOW WHEN TO LET GO

Let's consider an important question. Why did God create parents? We believe the answer is simple: God created parents in order to create human beings who don't need parents!

# THE IRONY OF THE PARENT-CHILD RELATIONSHIP IS THAT ITS ULTIMATE GOAL IS SEPARATION.

Rita and I want to grow closer and become more intimate as the years go by. We have become so dependent on one another that we cannot imagine life without each other. In contrast, the goal with our children is to love them to separation and independence.

One of the most difficult decisions any parent must make is when to "let go" and expect the child to move out into the world as a capable adult. Children begin their lives needing roots. The family provides this important part of their lives. But while they are becoming "rooted" in your family, you are also helping them to grow "wings." The day will come when you will need to help them pull up the roots and take to their wings.

When your child turns eighteen, you must work within the framework of a new philosophy that can be hard for some parents to accept. Your child might not do what *you* think is right, but they still have the right to do what *they* think is right!

*Let the discipline always match the offense.*
*—MARCUS CICERO, 43 B.C.*

Helping your child to become their own parent is one of the most important skills you will ever teach. Parents must give the world adults who are capable of making sound decisions, who contribute to society, and who further the Kingdom of God. But it's important to remember one thing.

YOU CANNOT TAKE ALL THE CREDIT, OR ALL THE BLAME, FOR WHAT YOUR CHILDREN BECOME.

In the wonderful book, *The Diary of Anne Frank*, Anne reflected on her father's attitude about child rearing. She wrote:

> Daddy used to say that children are responsible for a big part of their own upbringing. Parents can only give good advice or put them on the right paths, but the final forming of a person's character lies in their own hands.

Allowing mistakes is a key part of letting go of your child. Don't fault your children for a judgment call. You attempted to teach them good judgment, so you want them to use their own judgment. Celebrate it when they do.

Let Joshua 24:15 mark your home and family:
*As for me and my house, we will serve the Lord.*

*This is the true wisdom about love, to have, to hold, and, in time, to let go!*
—LAURENCE HOPE

# SUCCESSFUL FAMILIES UNDERSTAND AND PRACTICE THE OVERLOOKED SKILL OF COMMUNICATION

*The way of a fool is right in his own eyes but the wise will listen.*
—*Proverb 12:15*

Ask almost anyone what they believe to be the most important element in a successful marriage or family and they usually answer, "Communication." It's true. Without communication there can be no transfer of ideas or concepts, which is vitally important in a healthy family. Your dictionary would define the word "communication" as an impartation of information by means of speaking, writing, or using a common system of signs or behavior. Be assured that there is a lot of "imparting" going on today in marriages and families across America.

I (Richard) was in a counseling session a few years ago with a couple that was experiencing serious marital strife. A lot of information was being "imparted," but this couple was creating heat and not light. In a thankfully rare occurrence, the husband became so frustrated with his wife that he "communicated" his feelings by throwing a glass paperweight that had been lying on the conference table. It whistled by my head and made a huge dent in the wall. We got the message, almost too clearly. He was imparting information, but he was doing it in a destructive, self-defeating manner.

At this very moment, information, ideas, opinions, complaints, requests, replies, fears, words of love, words of joy, and expressions of need are flying through the air in personal encounters, on cell phones, and in e-mails! Passing information back and forth may be a dictionary's definition of communication, but it's not enough to get a bad marriage or troubled children back on track.

*In silent listening a man can be almost certain to improve his integrity.*
—*MEISTER ECKHART, 1362*

How we report what we hear depends on who we are.

Most families don't have a problem with *communication* as much as they have a problem with *listening*. Unless you make listening the most important element of communication, everything we're about to suggest in this chapter will be futile.

If your family is going to be successful, it's imperative that your family members communicate with each other. You'll only know what is going on in the mind of another by what they communicate to you. You may think you know your spouse or children so well that you know what they're thinking, but only God has that ability. I Corinthians 2:11 verifies this: *For who among men knows the thoughts of a man except the man's spirit within in him?"* (NIV).

There are two basic avenues for communication.

The first, *verbal* communication, is absolutely necessary in healthy relationships. It's the best way we learn what another is thinking, feeling, or experiencing. Families must make a commitment to communicate verbally, even if it is sometimes uncomfortable or painful. Good communication makes family members feel valued and may keep resentment and anger from building up and erupting at a later time. Families whose members don't talk don't know each other and won't have a way to understand one another or heal damaged relationships.

When communicating with your family, you must understand the power words and choose your words wisely, because they can either hurt or heal. In fact, the Bible states in Proverb 18:21 that words have the power of life and death.

Successful families communicate by using words that are first bathed in love. Good words are honest but also caring; calming, and not volatile; they are appropriate words, not curses or demeaning words.

The old saying, "Sticks and stones may break my bones, but words will never hurt me," is simply not true. One of the most poignant moments in our seminars occurs when we ask people to share words from their past that made a difference for them either negatively or positively. One middle-aged man spoke of an affirming little-league coach who had told him, "You can do it." One woman wept as she recalled being a sensitive ten-year-old whose critical grandmother told her, "You never do anything right."

Many people have stinging memories of words spoken decades ago either to them or about them that still cause deep pain.

An elementary school teacher once wrote on the blackboard the incomplete phrase, "Sticks and stones may break your bones, but words…" She asked her students to complete the last part in their own words. A six-year-old girl in the class turned in an all-too-true response: "Sticks and stones may break your bones, but words can break your heart." Don't think for a minute that words don't hurt. Children remember them for a lifetime. You still do, and your children are no different. Words can break a heart!

Hebrews 13:16 tells us we can make a sacrifice of words that pleases God greatly. Use the space below to note this sacrifice which benefits families as well.

_____

_____

According to Ephesians 4:29, only a certain type of communication should be spoken within the family. Complete the verse below.

*Let no _____ communication proceed out of your mouth, but that which is good to the use of _____, that it may minister _____ to the hearers.*

Our words can either wound family members or heal them. Describe from Proverb 12:18 the two radical outcomes caused by our words.

_____

_____

The second form of communication is *nonverbal* body language. We give each other non-verbal cues in relationships all the time. These may include posture, gestures, eye movement, or facial expressions. But we can only pick up certain clues from a person's behavior. It's impossible to know what another is thinking simply by looking at them. For example, Rita is a deeply caring person who comes to tears easily. Her tears have been misread by people who thought she was troubled or hurt, when her tears were actually a result of great joy or compassion. We only know for sure when she chooses to tell us what her tears mean. Never rely on nonverbal communication alone to determine another person's motives, feelings, or thoughts.

*I want you to destroy their communication systems. When they cannot talk to one another they will not be able to succeed against our forces.*

—*INSTRUCTIONS FROM PRESIDENT GEORGE H. BUSH TO GENERAL SCHWARZKOFF AT THE BEGINNING OF THE GULF WAR*

Communication is a circle of giving and receiving information. Information is given; information is received; a response is made; the cycle continues. *It is not enough that you allow a person to give you a message. You must respond to that message.* Healthy conversation involves giving and receiving statements that divulge thoughts, feelings, or values. Henry David Thoreau wrote, "It takes two to have a conversation. One to speak and the other to listen."

## FAMILIES USUALLY EXHIBIT ONE OF THREE COMMUNICATION STYLES:

**1. AGGRESSIVE COMMUNICATORS.** This family communicates by being rude to one another. They are bossy, overbearing people, and the words they use are selfish, accusing, and often volatile. Physical aggression may even be a characteristic of this nonfunctional family. Some members of the family never express their opinions out of fear of retaliation.

**2. PASSIVE COMMUNICATORS.** Communication is strained and rare in this family. Family members may be too shy or quiet and are often fearful of confrontation. Most often, there is apathy to the point that family members ignore each other or don't care to communicate with one another. This family isn't connected. There is little warmth because they don't know each other. Communication is only attempted in crisis situations or as a last resort.

**3. ASSERTIVE COMMUNICATORS.** This family makes communication a priority. Family members are free to express opinions and ideas. They are calm, confident, and want to understand what others are saying and meaning. They listen and respond to each other in appropriate ways. Each family member strives to respect the feelings and thoughts of the others.

Describe your family's communication style. Include ways in which you wish it could be improved.

_____

_____

List your family members, then note what you believe to be the most effective way of communicating with each. What does each member need most? Each responds most positively to what kind of communication?

_____

_____

Isaiah 40:3 explains that the Lord has given us a tongue for a specific purpose. Write that purpose.

_____

_____

## LEARNING TO LISTEN

The most overlooked skill in communication is the art of listening. Successful families have learned that communication only works when members learn to listen to each other. You've probably heard the adage, "God gave us two ears and one mouth, so He intended us to listen twice as much as we talk!" It's a good point.

Most people only listen in order to answer, attack, or defend. In fact, families are made up of basically four types of listeners.

**1. THE JUDGE.** The judge is the person in the family who believes they are always right. Their mind is already made up, so they see no benefit in listening to others. This person is usually negative and critical. They voice their opinion instead of listening.

Psalm 115:6 refers to this type of person. Complete the following verse.
*They have ears, but* _____ _____ _____.

**2. THE COUNSELOR.** The counselor listens only long enough to make a quick assessment and move on. This person is preoccupied with evaluating and offering advice that is usually not asked for. They accuse others of not listening. They only listen in order to dictate and tell others what should be done.
Proverb 18:13 refers to this person: *He that answereth a matter before he heareth it, it is folly and shame unto him.*

**3. THE INQUISITOR.** This person believes the way to listen is to constantly shoot questions at the other person or persons – something which can be tiresome and counterproductive. The inquisitor is prone to interrupt and is easily distracted. Asking questions in order to clarify understanding is important, but the inquisitor overdoes this tactic.

**4. THE GOOD LISTENER.** By far, the most effective listener in the family is the person who listens not only to the words being said, but who also tries to

*Listen for the sake of honor.*
—JOHN MILTON

understand the feelings of the person speaking. The listener pays close attention to body language, nonverbal signs, and facial expressions. The good listener is not judgmental of what is being said or how it is being expressed. The good listener's desire is to understand and respond accordingly.

Of the people you know personally, who is the best listener? Why do you enjoy being around them? List the reasons you think they are a good listener.

_____

_____

_____


The following verses describe the hindrances to good listening and communication. Write what you believe you need to personally apply from each.

Ephesians 4:25

_____

Colossians 3:8

_____

Proverb 11:12

_____

Proverb 12:16

_____

Proverb 15:5

_____

Proverb 18:23

_____

Proverb 25:24

_____

Proverb 29:20

_____

## THE SUCCESSFUL FAMILY LISTENS TO HEAR AND UNDERSTAND.

According to James 1:19, we should be quick to _____, slow to _____, and slow to _____.

*Go right on but listen as thou goest.*

—*DANTE*

A wonderful Chinese symbol, or pictograph, describes the effective listener. The symbol is a composite of four individual word characters: **ears** (we listen with our ears); **eyes** (we listen with our eyes); **heart** (we must listen with empathy); and **king** (we listen and then have the power of a king to act on what we have heard with effectiveness and power). Individually, each symbol carries its own definition and use; but when placed together, they become the single Chinese word meaning *listen.*

EAR — EYES — KING — HEART — **LISTEN**

This simple understanding of the ability to listen can be a powerful tool for any couple and family. If we begin to listen with our ears, eyes, and heart, and act compassionately, as a good king, we will see an overnight change in our families.

Read Proverb 20:12: *The hearing ear, and the seeing eye, the LORD hath made even both of them.*

Successful families have learned that we cannot really hear someone without listening to them. Effective listening is unselfish. It focuses on the other person's needs. The listener wants to understand what the speaker is saying, and why they are saying it.

The next time you're in a conversation, be a good listener. When you truly begin to listen, the results in your family will be long lasting. Members of successful families try harder to understand than to be understood. To do that takes listening. More than ever, families need to learn to practice the overlooked skill of communication – *listening*.

James 1:5 encourages us to ask God for wisdom, and assures us that God will give it to us liberally. Write a prayer below asking God for the direction and wisdom you need to become the listener that your family needs you to be.

*A bore is a person who talks when you wish he would listen.*

—*Ambrose Bierce, 1891*

Dear Father,

_____

_____

_____

_____

# CHAPTER 7

# SUCCESSFUL FAMILIES KNOW HOW TO HANDLE CONFLICT

*Be ye angry, and sin not.*
*—Ephesians 4:26*

All relationships have the potential for conflict. Conflict can best be defined as contention, disagreement, or a sharp contrast, between ideas, concepts, wishes, desires, or opinions. Conflict is a normal, natural part of life. As strange as it may seem, a life void of conflict is not healthy. Just remember this important principle:

## NOT ALL CONFLICT IS BAD

Conflict can teach us, strengthen our resolve, help us define our priorities, and build in us the skills necessary to disagree with civility. Anger may be the very thing which propels you and your family members to deal with issues that would be damaging to your family if left untended. A key scripture, Ephesians 4:26, helps us develop an important understanding regarding conflict: *Do not let the sun go down upon your wrath.* Normally this verse is understood to mean that you should not go to bed angry. Yet the writer, the apostle Paul, actually meant much more. Paul was presenting a more important and all-encompassing principle here. What he was actually saying to us about conflict is this:

## YOUR PROBLEMS WILL NOT GO AWAY IF YOU IGNORE THEM.

Don't run from your problems. Don't let the sky get dark in the west without taking care of these issues. Someone once said a problem completely understood is a problem half-solved. If you attempt to completely understand the conflict, then your potential for solving that conflict will be greatly enhanced.

*It is easier to stay out of conflict, that to get out!*
*—MARK TWAIN*

*He that hath no rule over his own spirit is like a city that is broken down, and without walls.*
*—PROVERBS 25:28*

Your greatest opportunities may come disguised as great problems with wonderful unseen benefits. Romans 8:28 really means what it says. All things *are* working together for your benefit.

Sometimes problems and conflicts are what take you where you need to be. You languish in apathy doing nothing, and suddenly a conflict wakes you from your slumber and you know you need to swim or you're going to sink! You find yourself in the midst of a storm and cry out to God to "calm the storm that is raging all around me!" God's reply is often, "I'm going to let the storm rage and calm you!" Think back to how many times you found you had learned valuable lessons and had become a better person after you successfully dealt with a conflict or problem. Remember that sense of satisfaction you felt? Of course you do.

God is constantly working to change, improve, and mature us. Conflict can do that very thing; it can be the friction which creates the motion that takes us forward. Don't run from the conflict and problems in your family. When you see a problem, flee, but always flee forward. Learn the important truths in this chapter so you will have the skills necessary to succeed in this area.

It is important for your family to remember that:

# CONFLICT IS NOT THE PROBLEM. THE REAL PROBLEM CAN BE THE WAY YOU HANDLE CONFLICT.

Anger is a completely normal reaction to conflict. Mismanagement of your anger is a problem. Conflict is a tool that can strengthen your family relationships and become a blessing to you. But you need to know how, according to God's plan, to handle conflict constructively. Most families allow conflict to destroy, degrade, and break down their relationships. That was not God's plan.

One unmistakable element of conflict is anger management. Ephesians 4:26 declares an important truth regarding anger: *Be ye angry, and sin not.* Notice that the verse implies that we will be angry at times. It's not possible to avoid this human response to life. Even Jesus became angry. Realize, however, that His anger had a method and reason. (Read Matthew 21:12.)

It is unhealthy to ignore or repress your anger. Anger is a natural response to fear, frustration, aggression, or anxiety which causes us to react in defense when threatened. It is as normal as hunger or thirst. Anger, however, demands closure. Without resolution we're left with a residue of pain which will decay even the most stalwart of personalities.

What does Proverb 16:18 say the sin is in anger? What is its result?

_____

_____

Many people seem to enjoy being angry. They lick their wounds, replay grievances long past, talk about the prospect of bitter confrontations still to come, and almost seem to savor their own pain and the pain they plan to cause others. The chief problem with this banquet of self-pity is that these people are devouring themselves. Destructive conflict, when unresolved and left to decay, will destroy a home and leave a marriage wasted in the wake of divorce.

*No lot is altogether always happy.*
—*HORACE*

It does not have to be so. Consider the statement of John Gottman, a psychologist at the University of Washington: "Anger and fighting are almost inevitable in marriage, but divorce isn't." For several years, Gottman and his associates studied 130 newlywed couples. They were able, with uncanny accuracy, to predict who would stay married and who would not. The predictor, Gottman wrote, is not whether a couple argues but whether the couple demeans, dishonors, or shows contempt for one another in those arguments. The best predictor of divorce is contempt, belligerence, and defensiveness toward one's mate and family. This is the key element that Gottman's research showed.[10]

Scripture does not say that conflict and anger are wrong. It tells us that the way we deal with conflict can be terribly wrong. We cannot resolve conflict with demeaning, hateful words or actions.

In Ephesians 4:26, Paul says that it is permissible and even healthy, at times, to be angry. The key is to display your anger in a constructive way. You must learn how to be honorable and respectful even in the midst of the emotion of family conflicts.

Read Ephesians 4:29-32.

What behavior should be eliminated when in conflict?

_____

_____

According to these verses, what behavior should be encouraged?

_____

_____

What is the resulting benefit from that behavior?

_____

_____

What does verse 31 say we are expected to control in our conflicts?

_____

_____

There are four possible responses to conflict. If you think about your family relationships, you will probably see these reflected in your own encounters where anger and frustration were present.

1. *I win; you lose.*
2. *You win; I lose.*
3. *We both lose, and no one wins.*
4. *Everyone wins, and no one loses.*

Your goal should be that everyone wins and no one loses.

Successful families have learned how to handle conflict constructively and fairly, and how to use times of conflict to strengthen and empower their family. Let's look at the principles they practice each day.

*The secret to family is to understand and accept that sometimes you have bad days and sometimes you have good days.*

*—KATHLEEN PARKER*

# Principles of
# Constructive Conflict

## Practice the Prevention Rule.

Rita and I discovered early in our marriage that we both *hated* conflict. We had grown up with unresolved conflict in each of our homes. Our families never seemed to get beyond the conflict surrounding the issue and come to a healthy resolution or closure. Benjamin Franklin was on target when he stated, "An ounce of prevention is worth a pound of cure." Too many families spend all their energy on the cure. If we would be wise enough to listen to God's Word, we would see how powerful this one principle happens to be. Just an ounce of understanding the concept of prevention could save pounds and pounds of failed cures.

*A quarrel is quickly settled if it is abandoned by one party – there is no quarrel without two.*

*—Seneca*

We must learn to resolve conflict before it starts. God's instruction on this point is clear.

> *The beginning of strife is like the letting of water. Stop the flow before it starts. Quit before the quarrel breaks out.*
> *—Proverb 17:14*

Once begun, the evolution of the conflict is incredibly hard to shut down.

According to Romans 14:19, we can prevent conflict by following after two things: things which make for _____, and things wherewith one may _____ another.

To further prevent conflict, Titus 3:9 instructs us to avoid _____ questions, and _____, and _____.

Why should we avoid these things according to this verse? _____.

Before we know it, conflict escalates into a full-blown confrontation. Our first response should be to consider what we're doing and why. The French philosopher and theologian, Jacques Predonie, admonished, "The greatest attack you can make on some problems and issues of conflict is to simply walk away from them and not turn back." His observations are right in line with

Scripture. Don't let conflict get started. Prevention is the most eloquent evidence of maturity.

Most of us can recognize conflict in its infancy. We have experienced those early moments when we begin to make choices that will either escalate the event or bring it to a reasonable conclusion and closure. We must be skilled enough to recognize the onset of conflict and to begin immediately to apply principles to make sure our decisions regarding our chosen behavior will be godly.

## LOOK FOR AREAS WHERE YOU ARE TO BLAME.

When you look for your responsibility in the conflict, it causes the other party to soften and often come to your defense. Ask yourself the following questions when you sense the conflict is about to start. They will help you apply the truth of Proverbs 17:14 and not allow the "water to begin flowing."

• **IS IT A WORTHY BATTLE?** Proverb 19:11
Is this really a big deal? Do you want to have conflict over this? Is it *really* worth the anxiety and agony? Anyone who has ever played basketball knows that during a game there is going to be what is called "incidental contact." Huge players running up and down a basketball court will bump into one another from time to time "incidentally." It doesn't affect the outcome of the game and should be ignored. It's not a real foul. The same applies in family conflict. In your family, learn to drop some things. Forget the incidental contact and go on with your day.

Proverb 26:21 describes what a contentious man is like. Write those characteristics here.

_____

_____

*None but the well-bred confess a fault or admit an error.*
—BENJAMIN FRANKLIN

• **AM I WRONG?**
Be quick to say "I was wrong." If you say that simple phrase to your family members, it will open a highway of opportunity for real discussion. If you are wrong, admit it. It isn't a big deal. Sometimes we're wrong. By admitting it, we will stop the flow of conflict...immediately.

Read James 5:16. What does this verse admonish you to do regarding conflict?

_____

_____

_____

Read Proverb 28:13. What is the consequence of covering your sin? What is the blessing when you confess it?

_____

_____

• **SHOULD I REACT OR RESPOND?**

I (Rita) hate snakes and spiders – and that can be a problem when you live out in the country as we do. One summer day, when I opened the backdoor of our home to take out the trash, there, sunning himself by the trash can, was a snake. I reacted! I began to scream for Richard, and I ran for my life.

When we react, we don't think, we just act! There is a huge difference between reacting and responding. To react requires no intelligence, only instinct. But to respond, you have to get that three-pound chunk of gray matter in your head involved. Responding requires time; it takes the facts. Only when you respond will you have a chance to resolve conflict.

I wasn't going to have a calm, reasonable discussion with anyone about that snake in our backyard. I had no interest in responding to the situation.

In conflict, too many of us react when we should respond. Be certain you respond; don't just react with a knee-jerk, thoughtless reply.

• **WHAT DIFFERENCE IS THIS GOING TO MAKE IN MY LIFE IN THREE DAYS? WHAT IMPACT WILL IT HAVE IN FIVE YEARS?** Many times, if you will ask these two questions, you'll find that what might have been a ridiculous conflict is simply not worth the battle in the scheme of the big picture.

*The art of being wise is the art of knowing what to overlook.*

*–WILLIAM JAMES, THE FATHER OF MODERN-DAY PSYCHOLOGY*

# PARENTS,
## IT'S IMPORTANT THAT YOUR CHILDREN SEE YOU EXPERIENCE AND THEN RESOLVE THE CONFLICT.

Many issues of family conflict seem to continue forever with nothing ever being resolved. Either people don't talk with one another or they keep fighting over and over about the same issues. Both parties think they're right and will fight to the end before giving up their position. In his classic book, *Brave New World*, Aldous Huxley made a very intriguing observation: "When two parties argue for an extended period of time, *both* are wrong."[11]

When arguments go on and on in front of the children with no resolution, both parents are wrong. But it's equally as wrong to let your children think you never have conflicts. How will they ever learn the right way to resolve conflicts? Certainly there are some issues which demand a private encounter behind closed doors. However, in the crush of day-to-day encounters and conflicts, children need to see their parents model the proper behavior necessary to resolve conflicts. It's the best laboratory they will ever have, and you are the teachers.

Philippians 2:14 admonishes us to do all things without _____ and _____.

Romans 12:18 directs us to live a certain lifestyle if at all possible. What does it say about how we should live?

_____

_____

## THERE ARE REALLY ONLY TWO CHOICES IN LIFE.

Early in our marriage, Rita was speaking at a women's conference when she made a simple yet profound statement: "We all live in only two worlds every moment of our lives. We either choose to live or act in **love**, or choose to live or act in **selfishness**. There are no other choices and no other options. Love or selfishness, the choice belongs to each of us on a **moment-by-moment** basis."

In discussing that statement later, we realized it is a key element in the success of a family against the potentially destructive onslaught of conflict.

Successful families have learned that important truth, and they practice it moment by moment. As simple as it seems, it is profoundly true. When conflict comes, they choose to act in love and not selfishness. Selfishness will destroy any family unit.

Read John 15:17. What does God command us to do in our relationships?

_____

_____


There are two evidences found in I John 2:5 that we are operating in love. What are they?

_____

_____

_____


The selfish person is characterized as being "rigidly right." Have you ever met such a person? Maybe there are members of your family who think they are always right and are so rigid about it they won't even consider the possibility that they might be in error.

It's a great tragedy to refuse to act in love and consider another person's opinion. Do you ever refuse to change and expect the other person to give in and see things your way?

_____

_____


According to Philippians 2:3, how should we esteem one another?

_____

_____

_____

_____


Read Ephesians 4:29 and then describe in your own words what you believe corrupt communication to be.

_____

_____

_____

*Sometimes the fact is that a family is more like a field of battle than a bed of roses.*

—Robert Louis Stevenson, 1881

We can live in love and reject selfishness by exhibiting the following characteristics.

• The members of a godly family that lives in love and not selfishness will listen to one another in order to *understand* what each other is saying, not to just defend their own position.

• The members of a godly family that lives in love will, in a potential conflict, remind themselves of a simple yet important fact: "Maybe he/she is right!" This simple mental exercise will cover a multitude of problems.

Read Matthew 5:25 to discover how conflict may quickly come to an end. Write it down here.

_____

Read Ecclesiastes 7:9. Write its principle here regarding conflict.

_____

Read Psalm 37:8 and Proverb 16:32 These verses outline the characteristics of a person who is successful in handling conflict. List these characteristics below.

_____

_____

## ARE YOU SELFISH?

When it comes to conflict, do you act like a baby? Babies can be the perfect picture of selfishness. Listed below are certain characteristics of babies. Check your "baby barometer." Consider the characteristics of a baby when it doesn't get its way. Do you see yourself reflected in any of these traits? Are you acting like an adult or a child?

### A BABY:
- Acts like he's the center of the universe and ignores everyone else.
- Is totally self-absorbed and selfish. If he's hungry that's all that matters.
- Expects you to take all the steps necessary to solve his problem. He doesn't do anything to contribute.
- Attempts to control you into submission by whining and complaining until you give in.

*A man is a fool who can't be angry, but is his wisest when he refuses to be angry. No man can humiliate me or disturb me unless I let him.*

*—BERNARD BARUCH*

Of course, babies are meant to act this way. But many families can't succeed because its members operate in this same childish selfishness. Remember, members of successful families understand the two important decisions they must make repeatedly every day regarding conflict: Will I act in love? And, will I act in selfishness? There are only two choices. No more. Your success depends on what you select.

## BE MORE CONCERNED WITH "HOW" YOU SAY THINGS RATHER THAN WITH "WHAT" YOU SAY

If you sit on a bench sometime at an amusement park and watch families walk by, you'll soon have a master's degree in human interaction. One family will be talking to each other with no conflict at all. Another family will be a "whirling dervish" of shouting and caustic remarks to one another over essentially the same issues. What's the difference? Is one family using different words? Are they speaking a different language? Hardly. Successful families can say almost anything to one another. The difference is, they concern themselves with one thing: It's not what they say to each other as much as how they say it.

I (Richard) learned years ago in our family that I could say something that might be essentially "correct," but the way I was saying it completely shut down the conversation. After Rita and I became aware of this important fact, we worked to turn it into a strength.

> When you say the *right thing* in the *wrong way*,
> it becomes the *wrong thing* to say even though
> it might be *right!*

We had to learn this important skill, and become role models for our children, under God's direction.

Here are a few suggestions as to how to say things more effectively to one another.

### • USE THE STILL, SMALL VOICE.

Read Proverb 15:1. How does the first part of the verse say we are to speak to one another? How are we instructed to not speak to one another?

_____

_____


We have seen parents scream and yell at their children, yet the kids seem to be deaf to every word. Many years ago, we discovered that if we got down close to the ear of our child and whispered, the power of those words was amazing. The spirit in your heart affects the tone of your voice. If you're filled with unresolved bitterness and resentment, it will come out in your voice.

Even God shouts His instructions to us in a "still, small voice" that is heard above all other sounds.

Lower your voice. Take a deep breath and speak in measured tones. If you're in a rage, step away and calm down. No one listens when you're shouting, but everyone does when you whisper.

Watch your body language and eye contact. A certain demeaning toss of the head or look in the eye can make the hearer angry and defensive.

• MAINTAIN YOUR SENSE OF HUMOR.

We can resolve many conflicts by simply allowing ourselves to laugh at the circumstance and at ourselves. Read Ecclesiastes 9:7 and Proverbs 15:13-15. What do these verses say a merry heart will do?

_____

_____

• DON'T GET PERSONAL.

Don't say irresponsible things about each other with the intent to hurt and demean. That's attacking the person, not the issue at hand.

• DON'T BRING UP THE PAST.

Don't bring up issues from the past and attempt to use them in the current conflict to win the verbal battle and bolster your position.

• DON'T GET OFF THE SUBJECT.

Don't get off the subject by widening your argument to issues unrelated to the current conflict and discussion.

## REMEMBER, HE WHO ANGERS YOU CONTROLS YOU.

Anyone can take away your freedom, but remember, the most important human freedom is your freedom to choose your attitude in any circumstance.

• AVOID STATEMENTS THAT ARE IMPOSSIBLE TO DEFEND.

One person may say, "I asked you to pick me up at school." The other may reply, "No, you didn't!" The first person responds, "Yes, I did!" This interaction is endless and fruitless. Make sure your statements are the truth.

- **AVOID SIX FATAL PHRASES:**

    1. "YOU ALWAYS…"

    No one always does anything.

    2. "YOU NEVER…"

    Again, you cannot accurately use the word "never" about another person's behavior or choices.

    3. "YOU SHOULD/COULD HAVE…"

    Stay out of the past. How can you rationally discuss something someone "should" have done? You can't go back. Operate in the present.

    4. "WHY DIDN'T YOU…"

    This statement is certainly not part of a good, healthy conversation. If you ask a person, "Why didn't you…?" there is no way they can "rewind" the experience and fix what they have already done. It is a waste of breath.

    5. "I WOULD HAVE…"

    Now you're getting arrogant. "I" would have done it this way or that way. "I" wouldn't have made that mistake. This remark only separates you and your listener even more and breaks down any chance for productive interaction.

    6. "YOU MAKE ME…"

    This one's a real dandy. Talk about taking away all responsibility for personal behavior. This statement is the king of them all! No one makes anyone else do anything. We choose. We are in control of our own actions and choices. Instead of saying, "You make me…," say to the other person, "I feel…," and explain your emotions from your perspective.

- **REPLACE THOSE SIX PHRASES WITH THESE.**

    1. "IN THE FUTURE…"

    This is a proactive statement. It gives both of you a positive position for a beneficial conversation and takes the defensiveness and sting of accusation out of your interaction. For example say: *"In the future, would you please leave my keys on my desk and not in the car?"*

*Quarrels would not last long if fault were only on one side.*

—*JEREMY TAYLOR*

## 2. "Next time…"

You cannot change what has already happened. There are no magic wands in families which will unspill the milk or magically erase a word or deed. For a more positive approach to how you say things, try this. For example, say: *"The next time you find out you will be late picking me up after work, I would really appreciate it if you would call and let me know."*

## 3. "What would have to happen…"

A person who is given the opportunity to think about their ideas, thoughts, position, or interest in a matter will be much more open to what you have to say. This phrase is one of our most important suggestions related to how you talk to someone. For example say: *"What would have to happen for you to be more helpful around the house with the children?*

**Anytime two people agree all the time about everything, one of them is unnecessary.**

In a family, it is both important and normal, to need to say some very personal and, often penetrating things. It isn't realistic to think that everything we ever have to say to each other will always be easy or comfortable. Say what you must say. Share expressions of your anger, hurt, disappointment, and frustration.

The key is to remember that it is not necessarily what you are saying, but the way you are saying it. Successful families know that key and use it every day to open the door of healthy communication and interaction.

Read I Peter 3:8-11. These verses reference several behaviors we should adopt in a conflict. Note the behaviors listed in each verse.

Verse 8:_____

Verse 9:_____

Verse 10:_____

Verse 11:_____

Complete Proverb 25:11: *A word fitly spoken is like*_____ *of* _____ *in* _____ *of* _____.

## UNDERSTAND AND KNOW HOW TO CONTROL DISPLACEMENT.

If you make time to re-read any section of this chapter for emphasis this is the one section we would suggest you memorize. We cannot think of a more important element or concept that has helped us to succeed in the area of resolving conflict in our family. It had its foundation in an event that occurred many years ago when we had been married for only a few months. I (Richard) came home from work and set my briefcase down on the coffee table. Rita, very harmlessly, said, "Richard, please don't set your briefcase on the coffee table. It scratches very easily." I became livid. "I don't need you to preach me a sermon about coffee tables," I ranted. "I work my fingers to the bone to buy you coffee tables, and I don't need to be chewed out for setting my briefcase down on your precious piece of furniture!" She looked at me with a justifiably stunned expression and asked, "What in the world is wrong with you?"

This is how conflict starts for most families. A simple event can escalate into World War III! The fact was my day had not gone well. If anything could have gone wrong, it did. Murphy's Law was in full stride from the broken copier to the meeting I missed because of the flat I had on the interstate. I wasn't mad at Rita. I was displacing my frustration on her instead of placing it where it belonged, on the bad events of my horrible day.

A familiar scenario regarding displacement is one in which Dad comes home from work after a horrible day and yells at his unsuspecting wife. His wife, still stinging from Dad's assault, yells at big brother about his messy room. Big brother, steamed by Mom's tirade, refuses to let his little sister use his bike to go to her friend's house as he had promised. Little Sis, totally unaware of the dynamic of human experience that has rolled down onto her, takes her frustration out on the family dog – who is totally confused as to what he's done since he was sound asleep on the rug in the den! The effect of displacement has hit this family in full force.

When we discovered the impact this phenomenon can have on a family we determined to not let it ruin our ability to get along and resolve conflict constructively. We established a set of "family frustration reporting rules" by which we still abide to this day. Here's how it works for us and can work for your family.

*Don't be angry you cannot make others as you wish them to be when you cannot even make yourself what you wish to be.*

—*Thomas A Kempis, 1471*

When I (Richard) served as chief of staff in the office of the lieutenant governor of Oklahoma, I had some pretty tough days. If I'd experienced one of those "barn-burner" days, instead of coming home and unloading on Rita, I would walk in the door and immediately report, "Honey, I had a wretched day at work. I'm not mad at you or anyone in the family. I simply don't want to be nice, cheery, or happy. I want to get my dinner, and watch the news, be a sourpuss for a while, and then get over it. It is not you; it's just been a really bad day." The amazing response was always the same. Rita, and often the kids, would reply, "I understand. How can I help? I can't believe how much you do with that job!"

## WITH AN UNDERSTANDING OF DISPLACEMENT, THE FAMILY WILL ATTACK ISSUES INSTEAD OF EACH OTHER

One night we had a family meeting about money. Things were a little tight at the time. Emotions were running high, and tempers were a bit short. I (Richard) felt that something had to be done. We were at each other's throats due to the short-term financial pressure, but I knew that everyone was not really mad at one another. I had the family sit around the dining-room table as I pulled out a dollar bill and placed it in front of them. I told everyone, "Guys, I know we aren't upset with one another. What we're really upset with is that dollar bill and the fact that we don't have enough of them right now. So, let's focus our anger where it really is...on the fact that we don't have enough of these guys." Everyone laughed and started yelling at the dollar bill. Then, with the tension relieved, we set a plan in motion to cover our needs and accomplish our goals together. We attacked the issue and not each other. It became a fun time for us all and one of our favorite family memories.

In dealing with conflict, Colossians 4:8 lists things we should eliminate. List them.

_____

_____

In contrast, Colossians 3:12-13 lists those things which are a part of constructive conflict. List them.

_____

_____

_____

It's a wonderful thing to avoid conflict. I once had a secretary who she said to

> Will your family be happy all the time? No. Sometimes there are things you need to be unhappy about.

me one day, "What most folks are fussin' about usually isn't what they're really fussin' about!"

Her statement is so true. In your family, sit down and discuss this important yet simple principle. Train yourselves in how to deal with displacement. You'll avoid tons of heartache and conflict with this one simple skill.

# HURT PEOPLE HURT PEOPLE

This principle regarding conflict has it roots in one of our weekend retreats many years ago. We were sitting on the patio of our room overlooking a beautiful golf course, deep in discussion about the rudeness of a young woman in our church. It seemed that every time any issue came up she had some caustic remark to make about the process or the committee. We had observed her with her children and saw her, under the veiled guise of being a "tough" parent, say such hurtful things that we were embarrassed for her kids.

Have you ever wondered why people do such hurtful things? The family unit is supposed to be the most supportive and loving place on the earth, but many times it is one of the most painful places many people can ever remember.

As we sat there sipping our coffee and allowing our thoughts to meander over this issue, it suddenly became very clear to both of us. Every person we had discussed and prayed for over the previous half hour had a single recurring characteristic. They had been hurt, or felt they had been hurt, by life – to the core of their very being. Others had hurt them and, consequently, the only way they knew how to deal with other people was to be hurtful themselves.

We discovered a principle that has helped us, and may be a big help to you as well, as you deal with the issue of conflict in your family and with others. When people are hurt, they often hurt others.

In Matthew 5:44, Jesus said our response to people who hurt us should be four things. Write them here.

1._____
2._____
3._____
4._____

Psalm 142:1-4 is the lament of a man deeply hurt. We all may encounter people

*When a conflict goes on for any extended period of time then everyone is wrong.*

—*SENECA*

each day who feel the same way. According to verse 4, how do they feel? How should we respond to them?

_____

_____

_____

What happens in most conflict situations?

*First, the conflict occurs.*
Some situation occurs which creates a conflict. There is broken fellowship, feelings are hurt, anger is present, and a full-blown disagreement is born.

*Next, a discourse takes place.*
We banter with each other as we jockey for position and try to get in the knockout punch. We talk (or shout) about the problem. Words are passed back and forth as we discuss what has happened. This phase of conflict can last for minutes or days, depending on the issue and the personalities involved. The worst thing that can happen, and it often does, is that no discourse takes place, and two angry people walk away with no closure. This is how families begin to drift apart.

*A resolution and some kind of attempt at closure takes place.*
At some point during the discourse, we arrive at an agreement as to how we will resolve the matter acceptably. Tempers have cooled, and clearer heads rule. We sincerely begin to try to work out the issue and come to an understanding. We arrive at the final element of our conflict. We have had the conflict and the discourse, and decided on an acceptable resolution; all we have left is one final step.

*Finally, an apology is offered.*
We attempt to say the right things, and we really mean them. We do the best we can to apologize and then go off to work, or head into the yard to mow the grass, or plop down in front of the television.

Have you ever noticed that after many arguments, you may think you've closed the issue but there still seems to be a residual malaise, a feeling that things still are not right? That now-missing element, which was present before the conflict began, is fellowship. If you haven't restored fellowship after family conflict, it's very difficult to go on. Everyone mopes about the house saying nothing. You drive to your favorite fast-food place, but don't say two words to each other on the way. You're supposed to have resolved the conflict, but fellowship hasn't been restored.

If handled correctly, properly resolved, and closed, conflict can make your family stronger, more mature, and even more supportive. Nothing is more productive in a family than for its members to realize that they can handle conflict and grow from the experience. Far too many families waste their conflicts by becoming bitter instead of becoming better!

But there is one more element, an element which is the most important part of conflict. Often totally overlooked, this final aspect is the hidden treasure of conflict. It caused our family to believe that we could handle anything that came our way. The element which we discovered is often overlooked and usually is not sought with all diligence, yet it is the most important.

*It is the healing.*

When healing comes after a conflict, you are stronger, more understanding of one another, more skilled in your relationships, and you have an accelerated love, trust, appreciation, and joy about being together. You begin to realize that you can overcome life's conflicts and that that sets you apart from most families.

When you cut your hand in an accident, the wound needs care. Once it has healed, the spot where the injury occurred is stronger than ever. A broken arm, once the bone is completely healed, is stronger at the point of the break than it was before the injury. Amazingly, this is exactly how it works with the family. When you find that healing has taken place, you're stronger than ever. It's God's wonderful plan for the power of productivity within conflict.

How do you start the healing process so the wound doesn't hurt any more? You must do several important things.

Colossians 3:13 says that we should forbear and forgive one another for what reason?

_____

_____

_____

You must remember five things in order to bring healing.

*Keep your eyes wide open before marriage and half-shut afterwards.*

—BENJAMIN FRANKLIN, "POOR RICHARD'S ALMANAC"

1. Forgiveness is the key to healing.
2. Forgiveness puts the other person first. Anger puts you first and closes the door to renewed fellowship and eventual healing.
3. Forgiveness is not forgetting what the other person did. Forgiveness is no longer holding that person accountable for the transgression.
4. Forgiveness blesses the other person. This will empower and energize our relationship. It will make you feel successful and in charge of your feelings.

Read I Peter 2:21-24 and write in your own words why and how a blessing is given.

_____

_____

5. Forgiveness should be verbalized. You must ask the other person to say the words, "I forgive you and accept your apology." If you simply ask, "Will you accept my apology?" the other person will probably say, "Yes." But you both need to say the words and then go on!

The way to close another person's spirit is to be harsh, belittle them, or refuse to admit you're wrong or have a part in the problem. To be sarcastic or rude to them in front of others, or to dishonor them, will shut down the possibility for closure and eventual healing.

Consider the psalmist who wrote in chapter 23, *"Thou preparest a table before me in the presence of mine enemies..."* (verse 5).

In our families, we must not see one another as enemies; we must learn to live together through forgetting and forgiveness.

When you hate someone, you are giving them power over you to control you. You have given them power over your sleep, your appetite, your health, your happiness, your joy, everything about you.

Read Proverb 10:12, which refers to the effects of hatred and love. Write them down below.

_____

_____

_____

When Jesus said, "Love your enemies," He was preaching sound ethics and good medicine. When He said, "Forgive seven times seventy," He was sharing with us the most important element in conflict resolution. Love one another. Make a conscious decision to do so. As the old saying goes, "You can be wronged or robbed in nothing unless you continue to remember it and harbor the ill."

*He who forgives ends the quarrel.*

—SENECA

# CHAPTER 8

# SUCCESSFUL FAMILIES ARE SPIRITUAL FAMILIES

*This book of the law shall not depart out of thy mouth; but thou shalt meditate therein day and night, that thou mayest observe to do according to all that is written therein: for then thou shalt make thy way prosperous, and then thou shalt have good success.*

*—Joshua 1:8*

God does not want your family to just work; He wants your family to *succeed!* Read Joshua 1:8 above and you'll see that God's plan for your family is *prosperity* and *success!* If you could only read one chapter in our book, this would be the chapter we would encourage you to study in depth with your family. However, these principles will only be successful if the Holy Spirit is operating in your hearts and lives.

*No nation can be destroyed that possesses good Christian homes.*

*—JOSIAH GILBERT HOLLAND*

Every family's first priority should be for each member to come to know Christ in an intimate relationship. The entire family will then benefit from the principles that should govern every relationship and situation.

The principles in each chapter of this study are all based on the four foundations we'll be studying in this chapter.

Write your definition of success.

_____

_____

How do you think the world defines success?

_____

_____

Successful families know that sometimes you have to set aside the "me" for the "we."

This next exercise will require 10-15 minutes of your time, but it's important to complete it before you go on. Read Ecclesiastes chapters 1-3. Then read chapters 5, 9, and 11. After you have finished reading those important chapters, read Ecclesiastes 12:13 and Joshua 22:5-6. On the basis of Ecclesiastes 12:13

and Joshua 22:5-6, coupled with the insight you have gained from the chapters you read in Ecclesiastes, write down God's definition of success:

_____

_____

_____

_____

Now that you've established how God views success you need to know what you must do to achieve that success. Let's look at the four important elements that make up the foundation on which a family builds their spiritual house.

## A SPIRITUAL FAMILY WORSHIPS TOGETHER.

The spiritual family chooses to attend and be involved in a church that teaches the uncompromised Word of God from the pulpit, from each Sunday school class, and from every platform of leadership. Their church strives to minister to the entire family; from the nursery department to the seniors programs, it is meeting the needs of people.

The church is friendly, open, and encourages fellowship. It's a church you want to invite others to attend. It's a church where your family can form lasting friendships and benefit eternally from fundamental, biblical, spiritual leadership.

Read Psalm 122:1. What does this verse say our response should be when we worship?

_____

## A SPIRITUAL FAMILY HONORS GOD'S WORD AND APPLIES IT IN THEIR HOME.

In Joshua 1:8 God promises that your family will be successful and prosper only if you are obedient to do three things. List those three things here.

1._____

2._____

3._____

The spiritual family teaches, reads aloud, discusses, and reveres the Word of God. They realize that nothing is more important than teaching God's Word in their home because it is alive, life-changing, and eternal.

Your children need to hear the Word and be aware of its power in their lives. You need to read the Word in your home, referring your children to the promises, warnings, and everlasting hope within its pages. Deuteronomy 6:6-9 instructs us to teach the Scripture by talking about it often.

When should you talk about the Word according to Deuteronomy 6:7?

_____

_____

## SCRIPTURE MUST BE SEEN AS WELL AS HEARD.

*Things that are holy are only revealed to those who are holy.*

*—HIPPOCRATES*

In our family we took Deuteronomy 6:9 literally. It reads, *"Thou shalt write them [the scriptures] upon the posts of thy house, and on thy gates."*

We posted Scripture all around our house. We placed key verses on our children's beds, and on the facings of our doors. At the front door of our home, visitors were greeted by an engraved brass plaque bearing the words of Joshua 24:15, *"But as for me and my house, we will serve the Lord."* It reminded us and all who saw it of the protection, healing, hope, and power of the Word of God that permeated our home. We knew we couldn't make it without the help of almighty God, and we were proud to say so to one another and to the world.

Keep the Word in written display in your home. It will aid your family with the important goal of memorizing Scripture.

A wonderful result comes from believing and living in the Word of God. See Deuteronomy 6:12. What does this verse declare that your house will be full of if you honor God's Word?

_____

Seek the help of your family in determining a family verse. This verse will be one for the entire household to memorize. Pray that this scripture will become cherished and carried into generations to come. Write it below.

_____

_____

_____

_____

## Spiritual Families Make Prayer a Daily Part of Their Home Life.

In our meetings, if we asked the question, "How many of you believe in the power of prayer?" we wouldn't be surprised to see most, if not all, of the people there raise their hands. Do you believe in prayer? If your answer is "Yes," then your answer to another question will give you real insight into your family life. That question is this: When was the last time you made time with your family, or in your own quiet time, to pray?

Many people remember a familiar slogan, "The family that prays together, stays together." The statement is more valid today than ever. It's difficult to find a family that has prayed together on a daily basis that has broken down or fallen apart. If you want your family to stay together, then pray together daily.

## THE PRAYERLESS FAMILY IS A POWERLESS FAMILY.

We want to be happy but don't want to concern ourselves with being holy. God loves us too much to allow us to be genuinely happy until we are genuinely holy.

In Colossians 1:9-14, the apostle Paul outlines in vivid detail how we are to pray for those we love. Use this system to direct your prayers for the members of your family. It is essential for every member of the family to know that every other member is praying for them in this way every day.

In Colossians 1:4, Paul mentions the love which Christians have for one another. He then expresses in verse 9, *"For this cause we also, since the day we heard it, do not cease to pray for you."* He then outlines how we are to pray for one another.

## Seven Ways We Are to Pray for One Another Every Day:

### 1. Pray That They Will Know God's Will. Verse 9

If you knew that every member of your family knew the will of God for their lives, wouldn't you be filled with peace and joy for them? Of course you would. We all want our family members to know God's plan. What does God want for them related to His will?

The final words of verse 9 make this clear.

• To have knowledge "...in all wisdom..." means to know what to do.
Read Proverb 3:21 in *The Living Bible*. Write how this verse defines wisdom and wisdom's two goals.

_____

_____

When you pray for your family members to know God's will, you are praying that they will be wise enough to know how to make good choices and do the right thing.

• To have knowledge "...and spiritual understanding;" means to know why to do it.
Read Proverbs 9:10-11 in *The Living Bible*. Write what those verses promise will be part of your life.

_____

_____

_____

To know the will of God is to have understanding. When you have understanding you know why you are doing the things you are doing.

### 2. PRAY THAT THEY WILL WALK WORTHY. Verse 10

According to language scholar Kenneth Wuest, the word "worthy" in this verse is a word which is best translated, "weight."

What you are praying according to this admonition then, is that your family members walk (go about their lives) each day in such a manner that their words and actions carry "weight." Have you ever said that someone's word "carries a lot of *weight*?" This is exactly what Paul meant.

We are to pray, "Lord, help my son (or other family member) live his life in such a way that he demonstrates the character of Christ and everyone who meets him knows that Your Word carries 'weight.'"

Read Proverbs 10:9. How does this verse describe a person who walks with "weight?"

_____

_____

### 3. PRAY THAT THEIR LIVES WILL BE FRUITFUL. Verse 10

God wants every family member to bear fruit in their lives. As you pray for your family members, ask that their lives be successful, beneficial to others, and meaningful. Fruit is an indication of accomplishment. Pray daily that in addition to a fruitful life, each member of your family comes to know the joy of achievement through effort and sacrifice which will ultimately become a blessing to others.

Read Isaiah 37:31. God's people will send _____ downward in order to produce _____ upward.

### 4. PRAY THAT THEY WILL HUNGER TO KNOW GOD. Verse 10

God wants to have an intimate relationship with each of His children. Psalm 4:3 says, *"Know that the Lord hath set apart him that is Godly for himself."* When each member of the family hungers to know God intimately, their potential for success in life finds daily partnership with the Heavenly Father! How wonderful it is to know each member of the family is growing in intimacy with Christ every day.

In Philippians 3:10, Paul affirms that to know God is to know two things. What are those two things?

_____

_____

### 5. PRAY THAT THEY WILL BE STRONG AND MIGHTY. Verse 11

What a wonderful thing to ask for your family! None of us wants our family members (especially our children) to be weak and easily tossed about by the challenges life brings. I (Richard) once heard the legendary Dallas Cowboys coach Tom Landry say, "Don't pray for an easy life. Pray to be a strong person." This is exactly what Scripture is admonishing here. Pray each day that your family will be able to make tough decisions based on God's principles and will be able to remain strong and mighty.

The key to being strong and mighty as expressed in verse 11, is to remember that your strength and might come *according to his glorious power!* Your prayer should be simply, "Lord, help each member of my family to be strong and mighty as they depend on You and Your Word, not on their own wisdom and strength."

Read Isaiah 40:29, Proverb 3:5, and Romans 13:1.

What three comparisons made between our human power and abilities and the power and abilities of God are discussed in these verses?

_____

_____

**6. Pray That They Will Be Patient, Persistent, and Joyous.** Verse 11b
The strength mentioned earlier in this verse has a beautiful result. You pray that your family, due to total dependence on God, will have three powerful characteristics in their lives.

• They will know God is at work and so they will be patient in life, not frantic and frustrated, living in a whirlwind of misguided passions.

• They will see God's hand in their lives and won't become fearful of His time-line. They will realize the power of persistence and how it is intimately tied to faith in God.

• There will be a joy in their lives that is a direct result of seeing God's miraculous hand in the events of each day. What a marvelous thing it is when you see your family joyous! C. S. Lewis made it clear when he said, "Joy is the most serious business of Heaven!"[12] Pray this joy into the lives of your family members each day.

Nehemiah 8:10 states, "The _____ of the Lord is your strength."

How can this source make us strong?

_____

_____

**7. Pray That They Will Express Thanks Each Day for the Three Greatest Gifts in Life.** Verses 12-14
Pray that your family members will always be thankful, every day of their lives, that they have been delivered from the awful penalty of sin. Everything else in life pales in comparison to the fact we have been redeemed by the sacrifice of Jesus Christ from an eternity of separation from God in hell.

We are to give thanks each day for three things:

• That we have been **delivered and rescued** from the penalty and power of sin. Satan will never have power over us again. Verse 13.

• That we have been **translated** into the kingdom of God for eternity (become eternal citizens of heaven with a new passport and identification!) Verse 13.

• That we have been **redeemed** through the shedding of His blood, and our sins are forgiven and never remembered anymore.

Paul instructs us to always remember with thanks what Christ did for us on the cross. We are to pray that our family will remember to be thankful for these things every day.

Read Matthew 16:26. What does this verse say is all that really matters in life?

_____

_____


Using the principles listed above, write a prayer for your family, which incorporates each element.

_____

_____

_____

_____

_____


Keep the copy of your prayer in a place where you can refer to it every day as you pray individually for each member of your family.

# SPIRITUAL FAMILIES BEAR SPIRITUAL FRUIT.

As a family continues to worship, study the Word of God, and pray for one another they become a Spirit-filled family. They begin to bear fruit as a result of the three foundational elements just studied. What are the fruits of a spiritual family?

### THE FRUIT OF LOVE

There is a desperate need for families to love and serve one another. As we have already discussed, love is the opposite of selfishness. The love needed in the family is the agape love of which Scripture speaks. Agape love is unconditional love. It is love for love's sake. It expects nothing in return. Only when members of a family are transformed by God's love will they be able to love in this divine way.

The attributes of this kind of love as displayed in a family are far-reaching. They are listed in I Corinthians 13:4-7. Read these verses and be reminded of the wonderful attributes of love.

Notice that the Word clearly commands us to "love" one another, but it never commands us to "like" one another. There will be times when we won't like each other. Our son once told his sister, "I love you, but I don't like you very much right now." That will happen. It's important to teach children to act in love, to do the right thing, even when it's difficult. Children must be taught the principles of loving each other even when they may not like each other.

One overlooked aspect of love is the seeking and giving of forgiveness. Love forgives and forgets. When our children were small, we taught them that merely saying they were sorry for an act was not enough. Sometimes they were sorry only that they were caught! We wanted them to see the value of seeking forgiveness. It is the loving thing to do to go to the person offended and ask for forgiveness. Is it difficult? Yes. But it's necessary to bring resolution and healing.

According to Luke 17:4, how many times should you forgive another when they ask for forgiveness?

_____

_____

_____

*The fruit of the spirit is love, joy, peace, longsuffering, gentleness, goodness, faith, meekness, temperance: against such there is no law.*
—*GALATIANS 5:22-25*

What is the principle reason we are to forgive one another? See Ephesians 4:32.

_____

_____

Paul wrote in II Corinthians 5:14 how "the love of Christ constraineth us." Determine the meaning of the word "constrain," then write how loving Christ would keep you from bringing harm, pain, or confusion to your family.

_____

_____

### THE FRUIT OF JOY

Children today may know a lot about happiness. They're happy at Christmas or on their birthday when they get presents. They're happy that Daddy is home or Mom made cookies. But the principle of joy is different. It is a spiritual attribute that parents who have learned how to live joyously in an often chaotic, unsettled world must exemplify and teach their children.

Joy is more than happiness or just being content and satisfied. Happiness fades away. Happiness depends on "happenings;" joy lasts forever. Joy doesn't waver. It's present when happiness is not. It can be there during the darkest, most difficult days.

Only spiritual parents can teach the principles of spiritual joy. Joy is an every day evidence, a testimony that we walk with Christ. Joy should be a daily principle that verifies to the family that God rules their hearts and lives. Nothing should shake it. It's an attitude of the heart!

The following are references to "joy" in the New Testament. Read each, then write the reason for the expressed joy in each verse.

*One must not think about what he should do, but about what he should be.*

—MEISTER ECKERT

Romans 5:11

_____

Philippians 1:25

_____

Nehemiah 8:10

_____

I Thessalonians 2:19

_____

Psalm 16:11

_____

Philippians 4:1

_____

There are also verses that declare we can have joy in spite of situations or circumstances. Read the verses below and complete each one.

_My brethren, count it all joy when ye fall into divers_ _____.
James 1:2

_I am filled with comfort, I am exceeding joyful in all our_ _____.
II Corinthians 7:4

### THE FRUIT OF PEACE

Like joy, peace is a spiritual principle that comes through perfect confidence in God's love and protection. Many homes are anything but peaceful. It's your responsibility as a parent to maintain a peaceful home in the midst of conflict or difficulty. Peace is a choice. You choose daily to react to life in a frenzy or calmly, through faith or fear, worry or peace.

A favorite story we shared with our children regarding peace is the moving story of Corrie Ten Boom, who was a prisoner of war in a Nazi concentration camp during World War II. Corrie's sister died in the camp, and at one point other prisoners criticized Corrie's stubborn will to rejoice and be at peace despite the unfathomable cruelty. The Scripture verse that she quoted over and over during those dark, dreadful days was Isaiah 26:3:

_Thou wilt keep him in perfect peace, whose mind is fixed on Thee._

The secret of peace of mind is a fixed mind. It's concentrating not on our circumstances, but on who God is and who we are to Him. Praise God we can teach our children the principle of personal peace in every situation of life.

In John 14:27, Jesus said He gives us peace that is different from the world's peace. Describe those differences.

_____

_____

### THE FRUIT OF PATIENCE

Americans are impatient people who live in a world of instant-everything. Our children are exposed to fast food, fast computers, and instant gratification. Patience is not a virtue that is strictly taught. However, the benefits of patience can be lifelong, and the difference sometimes between success and failure.

## ONE OF THE MOST IMPORTANT SKILLS YOU CAN TEACH YOUR FAMILY IS THE ABILITY TO DELAY GRATIFICATION.

Patience, defined spiritually, isn't just the ability to wait; it's usually the choice to delay your own pleasure or satisfaction for a greater good. It's choosing to reject acting rashly or foolishly until you've learned all the facts. It's seeking God's will in a matter, and waiting until you're sure it's His will and not your own before you act. You teach your child to be patient by being patient yourself. Children need to see Mom and Dad delay personal wants until the budget allows them to have them. They need to hear why they must wait to have something until they help earn the money to pay for it.

It's also healthy for a child to learn patience with other people. To listen intently, to wait until they have understood before they react, to wait to play with toys until other children or siblings are finished playing with them, all are lessons in patience. Patience is a principle that will give your child balance throughout his entire life.

Read Romans 5:3 and James 1:4. Then ask each family member to recall a time when having patience proved to be the wisest action.

### THE FRUIT OF KINDNESS

Kindness, plainly and simply, is being interested in the needs, the hurts, and the lives of others before your own. Kindness is a godly trait that you can develop in your home by teaching your children to be Christlike. In situations that call for a choice between kindness and selfishness, ask your children, "What do you think Jesus would do here?" We did – long before it became a "catch phrase" in the '90s. It works. Never pose the question in a judgmental, condemning tone. Just ask. Leave the answer to them.

Kindness is not only the ability to recognize other's needs, it's also the quality that spurs us to act on those needs. Teach your children how to continually be looking for needs that they can help meet. The elderly neighbor who has difficulty getting her mail everyday from the mailbox, the single mother who needs to go to the grocery store but whose child is sick, the new student at school who needs a friend – each of these is yearning for someone's kindness. Teach your children that they can be the ones who care in Jesus' name.

Read II Corinthians 6:6 with your family. Determine that your family will perform one act of kindness together every day for one week. List them here.

1._____
2._____
3._____
4._____
5._____
6._____
7._____

## THE FRUIT OF GOODNESS

You have a wonderful opportunity to instill a desire for goodness in your children. Goodness is the desire to live clean, honorable, kind, wholesome lives. Obviously, our human nature leans toward the opposite. University of Oklahoma assistant football coach Brent Venables said of one of his star players, Rocky Calmus, the 2001 Butkis Award Winner, "We'll miss Rocky. He's a great player, but mostly he's a good, good man." What a legacy this young man is already building!

What are some of the qualities of people who are perceived as being "good" persons? They are thoughtful of others, obedient, humble, respectful, honest, and unselfish. Notice these qualities in your children and applaud and reinforce them. As soon as your children can understand the concept, connect goodness to doing godly things. However, be sure to teach them that goodness alone doesn't buy salvation; that salvation is a gift that depends not on our goodness, but on the goodness of God.

Without God at its center, a family is only a three-ring circus; engagement ring, wedding ring, and suffering.

According to II Thessalonians 1:11, Paul prayed in a specific manner for the church at Thessalonica. What did he ask of God?

_____

_____

Second Thessalonians 1:12 states the purpose of goodness. Write it here.

_____

_____

### THE FRUIT OF FAITHFULNESS

When I (Rita) was about six years old, I had a spiritual experience that has always been very dear to me. While staying with my grandmother, I noticed an embroidered wallhanging with a verse from Hebrews 11:6 that said, "Without faith it is impossible to please God." It bothered me that I didn't understand the word "faith" because I certainly wanted to please God. That night before going to sleep I asked God, in my childlike way, to show me the meaning of the word. As I lay down on my pillow, the words exploded in my spirit, "Faith means to believe." That's it! It is simple and true. It pleases God when we believe.

Faithfulness is the result of being "full" of believing in Him. Families should rely on Christ by trusting and believing what His Word says, what He speaks directly to them, and how He answers prayer. Faithfulness is the result of being totally consumed with believing in God the Father and His Son, Jesus Christ. Nothing is more important than what your family believes. What you believe determines who you are.

Using Hebrews 11:1, 6, write a family prayer list of things for which you will pray faithfully until they come to fruition. Refer to this list often as you pray together, always remembering that the reward of faithfulness is answered prayer.

_____

_____

### THE FRUIT OF GENTLENESS

The world can be harsh. Gentle people, especially young men who are tender or merciful, are often thought of as "weak." Yet nothing could be further from the truth. It takes a real man, a strong man, to be self-controlled, disciplined, and kind.

To be gentle means to be mild, not severe, rough, or violent, but tender and merciful. On occasion parents need to use firm discipline, but even then children need the "spirit of gentleness." Make sure that after every encounter discipline, you spend at least the same amount of time loving, holding, and softly telling the child how much you value and love them.

We once asked teens attending a youth retreat what they would change most about their family. The number one answer was, "I want my parents to stop yelling at each other and us." Shouting, yelling, cursing, or name calling has no place in the Christian home – a home that is trying to emulate the spirit of gentleness. Rita often tells women that the most beautiful, soothing, comforting sound children should hear should be the sound of their mother's voice.

Fill in the blanks from II Timothy 2:24.

*The servant of the Lord must not* _____; *but be*

_____ *unto all* _____.

### THE FRUIT OF SELF-CONTROL

We live in a society that doesn't promote self-control. In fact it encourages us to live unrestrained, self-serving lifestyles. We're taught to believe we deserve the best, the most, and the greatest. Our society's motto has become, "Deny yourself nothing, especially sexual or material pleasures." This philosophy flies in the face of the Christian lifestyle, which is one of restraint and self-control.

*Do your duty and leave the rest to heaven.*

*—PIERRE CORNIELLE, 1636*

Children who are not taught self-control at home will seek more and more stimulation for fulfillment. They don't care about the consequences of their actions. All that matters is that they get what they want.

Today we are seeing children who are no longer guided by a conscience. It is nonexistent. Why? They have no self-control. When children are not taught self-control in anger management, they have no regard for authority or discipline. The statistics of children committing serious crimes has risen sharply. Could it be directly tied to children who have not been taught the godly principle of self-control?

Read Proverb 25:28 to determine what a person must rule in order to have self-control. Write it here.

_____

This verse refers to the fact that walls, which surrounded cities, protected the occupants from enemies who would kill and destroy them. If we do not have the "wall" of protection (self-control) we are defenseless against the attack of our enemy, Satan, who seeks to destroy us. (See John 10:10.)

Matthew 7:24 reminds us that the wise man builds his house upon the rock. Spiritual families build their lives on the foundation of worship, God's Word, prayer, and spiritual fruit.

Build your house upon a sure foundation so that when the storms of life come – and they will come – your family will not just survive, it will succeed!

# CHAPTER 9

# SUCCESSFUL FAMILIES KNOW THE TRUTH ABOUT MONEY

*Where your treasure is, there will your heart be also.*
—Matthew 6:21

"Show me the money!" The phrase made popular by the movie *Jerry Maguire* is the motto of this generation.

It's true, it takes money to eat and to pay the rent, the IRS, the grocer, the gas station, and the electric company, just to name a few. But the authors of the book, *The Day America Told the Truth* discovered some disturbing trends in their research. When Americans were asked, "What would you give up to get ten million dollars?" 25 percent said they would abandon their family forever; 25 percent said they would abandon God and the church; 16 percent said they would leave their wife. In many homes, money has become king.[13]

It's a well-documented fact that many couples separate and eventually divorce due to how they view and respond to money issues. If you think politics and religion can be controversial, money, or the lack of it, can light the fuse to a bomb whose explosion often rocks the family to its very foundations.

If a terrible disease was ravaging members of your family wouldn't you get help immediately? Money problems are a result of character issues and are a cancer that is tearing at the very core of family unity. Families should not allow this to go on unchecked.

God is very interested in this issue as well. In the Bible there are more than 500 verses about prayer, and around 500 verses that discuss faith, but there are more than 2,000 references to money and possessions! Of the 38 parables in the Bible, 16 of them, almost half, are about money.

*There can be no freedom or beauty about a home that depends on borrowing and on debt.*
—HENRIK IBSEN

*A man who is satisfied is a man who is well paid.*
—SHAKESPEARE

Matthew 6:21 tells us that there will always be a powerful tension between our possessions and priorities. Read the verse and then write why you think the heart is so easily deceived.

_____

_____

God knows that money is the hardest thing you will ever give up. Have you ever heard anyone say, "It's not the money, it's the principle of the thing." You can be sure, *it's the money*!

In this chapter, we will study principles which will help you determine what God says should be important to you in terms of your finances. In addition, we'll see how to make some realistic plans.

# PERSPECTIVES ABOUT MONEY

The pursuit of wealth and so-called "financial independence" has become a priority in many American families.

Almost every decision made in the family – including time involvement, friends, activities, and day-to-day choices – is determined by money.

*So little in his purse and so much on his back*
—*JOSEPH HALL, 1656*

In the Broadway musical *Fiddler on the Roof*, Tevye, the father, sang, "If I were a rich man." Today, many sing the same song, complaining to God, family, and friends that "if we were only rich" their problems would vanish.

Ecclesiastes 5:10-12 gives us a clear, if not readily believed, answer to this problem. What do these verses say would happen in our lives if we were granted our wish for riches?

_____

_____

_____

Read Deuteronomy 8:17-18. According to this verse, who ultimately gives the power to receive wealth? Why?

_____

_____

Many people believe money will take away every pain and sorrow. They see it as an anesthetic, an aphrodisiac, and a tool to use to wield power over others.

Read Job 31:24-28 to discover the result of making gold (money) your hope. Write it here.

_____

_____

Money is simply a form of energy. It can be the source of great pleasure or the undoing of what began as a wonderful, harmonious marriage. There are only six things you can do with money:

- Give it away.
- Save it.
- Invest it.
- Hoard it.
- Lend it.
- Spend it.

Notice that spending is last on the list. Spending should never be the first thing you do with your money.

*I can seem to get no remedy from the consumption of my purse. Borrowing only lingers and lingers it out and the disease seems incurable!*
—SHAKESPEARE, "KING HENRY"

## MONEY IS POWER, FREEDOM, A CUSHION, THE ROOT OF ALL EVIL, AND THE SUM OF ALL BLESSINGS.
### —CARL SANDBURG

Is money "the root of all evil" as Sandburg wrote? Read I Timothy 6:10 and write what Scripture says regarding that statement.

_____

_____

_____

_____

Read Job 31:24-28 and Proverb 23:5. These verses destroy the myth that money will solve our problems. According to these passages, what really happens to money?

_____

_____

Contrast Proverb 11:28 with Proverbs 3:13-14. What do these verses say our main pursuit in life should be?

_____

_____

Proverbs 22:1, 4 describe real wealth. Write what each verse declares is more important than riches.

_____

_____

Many families will do anything to "keep up with the Joneses." But parents send a dangerous message to their children this way. They demonstrate, by their own driving passion and selfish pursuit of money, that money is more important than anything, and as far as they're concerned, they deserve everything money can buy.

They're always looking for more: the highest, the greatest, the latest, the best, the most popular, or whatever the television tells them they cannot do without.

The American advertising industry has learned how to skillfully manipulate this character flaw in the American public, keeping us dissatisfied and on the hunt for more and better material possessions.

It should be no surprise that today's children have learned the price of everything and the value of nothing.

According to Hebrews 13:5, what should we be teaching our children about the accumulation of wealth?

_____

_____

_____

First Timothy 6:6-10 teaches us that there is a cost to loving money. What is that cost?

_____

_____

Read I Timothy 6:17-19. Contrast the impact of riches described in verse 17 with God's plan for riches as expressed in verses 18-19.

_____

_____

Read II Chronicles 31: 20-21 and list the four ways King Hezekiah demonstrated the biblical view of prosperity.

1._____

2._____

3._____

4._____

## THE ANATOMY OF FINANCIAL PROBLEMS.

Financial difficulties in families can place a strain upon relationships which can lead to tremendous problems. Many of you have found yourself in that position of terror. That's right, terror. Not fear, anxiety, or despair, but terror. Money problems will do this to you. Perhaps you're there right now, at this very moment. You have no interest in discussing or even thinking about the other ten reasons families succeed. You may have scanned the table of contents of this book and turned immediately to this chapter looking for guidance. You don't know what to do, and you see no way out.

In the movie *It's a Wonderful Life*, George Bailey, who had financial problems, wished he had never been born. Some of you may feel the same way. You may have thought that life was not worth living. You've felt anger, shame, resentment, and more emotions than you can list. The bills continue to mount. The mailbox is a growling monster filled each day with window envelopes. You stuff unopened bills in drawers with the hope that the "out-of-sight-out-of-mind" principle will somehow make them magically go away.

Money should not be the root of all evil; it should be the root of all good.

You didn't sit down some months or years ago and decide you were going to bring your business, farm, or family finances to their current state; but here you are in the middle of a financial nightmare with all the accompanying terror and pain. Sleepless nights, fear, and paranoia grip you constantly. You've lain awake at night looking up at the ceiling thinking as King David in the Old Testament who lamented, *"Oh that I had wings like a dove! For then would I fly away, and be at rest!"* (Psalm 55:6).

How did this happen? you wonder. Guilt rages in your spirit accompanied by anger and resentment. No one else, you believe, has this kind of horrible existence. Life is just not fair.

Debt is like a cancer. At first it occupies only a small part of the body. But it never stays small unless you control it. How can a family or marriage survive when financial pressure hangs over them each day?

According to legend, Dionysius the Elder, who lived in Sicily from 405 to 367 B.C., wanted to prove a point about the pressure of the unpredictability of life. His servant, Damocles, assured Dionysius that nothing would disturb his inner peace and ability to deal with the world. Dionysius set out to prove him wrong. Dionysius invited Damocles to a sumptuous banquet and seated him beneath a sword that was suspended from the ceiling by a single strand of thread. Dionysius made his point. Damocles could not think, eat, or enjoy a single moment of the feast with the sword hanging inches over his head. He knew that at any moment the strand could break and plunge the sword into his neck, taking his life.

Maybe you've heard the story of Damocles' sword. You may have even related this legend to your own situation. Do you feel this uneasiness about your finances? Are you waiting for the "sword to fall" and send your family into ruin? Are you considering bankruptcy? Do you feel at fault?

Money issues are some of the most critical issues in a marriage and family. Until you find peace in this area, nothing else will seem to work. The "Damocles sword" will hang over your head and disrupt every decent moment you try to have with your family.

Let us assure you, if you're at this point, or have ever been, we know exactly how you feel. When we lost our business in the early '80s during the oil downturn, we lost everything. Because of some business decisions that didn't turn out well, not only did we lose our shirts, we lost our whole wardrobe. We weren't sure how we would make our employee payroll or even meet the most basic needs of our family. It was horrifying, nightmarish ground we were walking on.

God provided for us then, and He will provide for you now! There is not one single reason you and God cannot turn this thing around. It may take time, but you can do it. We did it. Others have done it. And by the grace and help of God, you do it can too! The principles you learn in this chapter will be a start.

If you aren't married and are reading this book to prepare for marriage, wonderful! You have an advantage over those of us who had to learn the hard way in the college of hard knocks. We know many alumni of that school!

If you're in the midst of a financial crisis, read on and take heart. You can do it. Take personal responsibility, coupled with immediate, reasonable action. You can remain stagnant and frozen with fear, or you can do the hardest and most important thing you have ever done in your life. Take God's Word and these principles to heart, and get after it!

Remember, although it's certainly true that money won't buy happiness or peace of mind, neither will poverty and despair. God doesn't want you to think He dispenses righteousness on the heels of lack. He wants to meet your every need, and then bless you with more. However, His great desire is for you to allow Him to control your resources, as you are stewards of what belongs to Him. It's a matter of trust.

## TAKE THIS SIMPLE TEST TO SEE IF YOUR FAMILY MIGHT BE IN FINANCIAL TROUBLE.

1. Do you usually use credit cards to finish out each month?
2. Do you ever pay your bills late?
3. Do you float funds from expense accounts, etc., to pay your bills?
4. Do you ever hate to hear the phone ring?
5. Do you always pay the minimum payment on your credit cards?
6. Do you never tithe or make a charitable gift?
7. Is a savings or retirement account non-existent?
8. Have you had more than one overdraft check on your bank account this past year?
9. Do you dream of getting rich quickly?

If you answered "yes" to three or more of the above questions, you're living on the edge of disaster.

*It is impossible to drain the swamp when you are constantly fighting off the alligators.*

*—ANONYMOUS*

Proverb 21:20 states that *in the house of the wise are stores of choice food and oil* (NIV). Write down what a foolish family will do with those resources.

_____

_____

_____

Luke 14:28-30 admonishes a family to prepare financially. Write these instructions in your own words.

_____

_____

_____

Don't expect overnight miracles from these, or any, principles related to financial problems. An aircraft carrier cannot turn on a dime. It takes miles for the huge craft to slow down and then make a long sweeping turn to go in the opposite direction. Solving your family financial problems might be a similar situation. Get together with your whole family and have a meeting to discuss turning the ship around. The problem is affecting everyone, so everyone needs to get on board in the solution process. Swallow your pride and get with a program that you design for your needs. Start the aircraft carrier of your finances moving in the right direction. It took us years to turn things around where it may take you months, or maybe only days. Whatever the case, the most important thing is to get a plan and start.

## THE BIBLICAL PERSPECTIVE OF MONEY.

*What is the greatest law concerning money? Whatever you have, spend less.*

—SAMUEL JOHNSON, 1782

God wants to bless you, to build a hedge of protection around you, and take care of you in such a way that the people around you see His blessing and want to know Him as well. Nate Saint, the martyred missionary to the Auca Indians of Ecuador said it clearly,[14]

# LORD, I PRAY THAT I MAY BE PROSPEROUS, NOT TO SIMPLY BE RICH, BUT TO DEMONSTRATE THE VALUE OF KNOWING GOD!

God challenges you to test Him in this area. In fact, Malachi 3:10 is the only time in Scripture God tells us to test Him. The scripture reminds us not to worry about our needs. God will provide as a loving Father. If He takes care of the birds of the air and the creatures of the field, He will certainly take care of you. That's His promise. God wants to be in partnership with you regarding money.

Read Psalm 37:25. From what does the verse say God will protect His children?

_____

_____


Read Isaiah 45:11. It is one of the most remarkable verses in the Bible. In this verse, what does God declare we are to do regarding the promises He makes to us?

_____

_____


# GOD HAS A FINANCIAL PLAN TO SET YOUR FAMILY FREE!

Before you continue with this section, read Deuteronomy 11:26-28. These verses speak of blessings and curses.


What do the verses say bring God's blessings?

_____

_____


What do the verses say bring God's curses?

_____

_____


There are five steps to God's financial plan for your family.


## 1. TRANSFER OWNERSHIP OF EVERYTHING TO GOD.

Mine. Ours. Over twenty years ago, these words described our attitude regarding the subject of money. It belonged to us. Then we heard a message on the subject of finances that changed our lives forever.

Before hearing the message, we usually nodded in God's direction regarding money, but we still felt it was ours. We didn't give with joy or celebration, and we only "tipped" God at church. We had an attitude much like the Virginia rancher portrayed by Jimmy Stewart in the Civil War movie, *Shenandoah,* when he offered a blessing at dinner. "Lord," he began, "We tilled the land, raised the cattle, and planted the seed that put the food on this table. We did it all by our own toil and sweat. But, we want to thank You anyway. Amen."

Is that your mindset, too – thinking you own the things you have, when in reality they're all gifts on loan from God?

I (Richard) recall watching a television interview of a famous country music star. In relating how he operated his band he joked, "We operate by the golden rule. I've got the gold, so I make the rules!" I don't think he was kidding.

If you believe the resources you have are yours then you will make the rules as to how those resources are used. Before you ever find success, you must accept and trust the One who really does own the gold.

Read Haggai 2:8. What does it make very clear about wealth?

_____

_____

That day over twenty years ago, as we drove along the highway discussing the message we had just heard, our hearts were convicted, and we knew we had been seeing everything from the wrong perspective. Nothing really belonged to us. Our house, cars, clothing, children, and jobs were all gifts from a loving father and we were simply stewards of those gifts.

A steward knows that his responsibility is to care for the possessions of the owner. He never sees them as his own. God gives to us not so we can possess, keep, and hoard them, but so that we can be vessels and pipelines of His blessing to others. When we are trustworthy, it makes it possible for Him to bless us even more. His ownership has a single goal: to use all of His resources to be a blessing to His children.

Read Luke 12:41-48. Write the five characteristics of a good steward expressed in those verses.

1._____

2._____

3._____

4._____

5._____

As soon as we arrived home that day, we put the children down for their naps, and in a lifechanging meeting at our dining room table we transferred ownership of everything back to God.

Read the following verses in Malachi and write the reason God was upset with His children.

1:6-8        They didn't put God first in their _____.

2:14-16      They didn't put God first in their _____.

3:7-9        They didn't put God first in their _____.

Read Matthew 6:33. Why does God want to be in first place in our lives?

_____

_____

We sat down at our old IBM typewriter, and in the most official-sounding legalese we could think of, we wrote a document that rivaled the Magna Carta and the Declaration of Independence in its scope and authority! On that sheet of paper we listed *everything* God had given us and left places at the bottom for our signatures and the date which to us "authorized" the transfer of all ownership. After praying together, we signed the document, declaring ourselves to be accountants and stewards of God's resources and His gifts.

We were free. It wasn't our money anymore; it was His, and our responsibility was now very simple. Obey His instructions. From that moment, every decision we have made about money have been made on the basis of His will and ownership.

*It is difficult to think nobly when all one can think about is making a living.*

—JACQUES ROSSEAU, 1762

Complete I Chronicles 29:11.

"*Thine, O LORD, is the greatness, and the power, and the victory, and the majesty: for* _____ *that is in the* _____ *and in the* _____
*is*_____.

We suggest that the head of the home sit down with the family and have a similar "Independence Day" ceremony with a document of your own creation. It will change your lives and open blessings from God's storehouse that you've never imagined.

## 2. TITHE AND GIVE OFFERINGS JOYOUSLY.

Isn't it amazing how tons of metal and wire can fly six hundred miles an hour at an altitude of 35,000 feet! Or that cell phones allow us to talk across thousands of miles as clearly as if we were sitting next to the other person? Automobiles. Radio. Television. Microwaves. Computers. The Internet. So many things in our daily lives work without us really having a clue as to how they function. We just know they do.

Tithing is like that. You don't have to understand all about how it works; you just need to know that it does.

Before dialing your cell phone or starting the car, you don't pray with focused passion that they will work. You accept their function by faith. That faith is a result of hundreds of successful experiences.

The same is true for God's principles. Read and then trust His directions. With each success, you'll gain more experience and the confidence to do more. The problem with many people is that they've never stepped out in faith and proven God in the area of finances. You'll find a key word for understanding this concept in the following passage.

Read II Corinthians 9:6-8. God "prefers" our giving and tithing to be accompanied by which characteristic?

_____

_____

God prefers a child who will be joyful about obedience. It is the greatest sign of trust and love.

When our children were young and we instructed them to make their beds or take a bath, we always appreciated cheerful obedience. On the occasions that *joyful* obedience was not present, we still expected and accepted *simple* obedience. Why? We knew, as God knows, that while our children were displaying simple obedience they were learning the discipline and skills that would one day result in joyful obedience.

Let's discuss several important principles about tithing and giving offerings.

• TEN PERCENT MEANS TEN PERCENT.

The word "tithe" means "ten." God has instructed us to bring 10 percent to Him. Some people ask us if they should give 10 percent of their gross income (before taxes) or 10 percent of their net income (after taxes). Our answer is usually the same. It depends on whether you want a gross blessing or a net blessing! That decision, as you will see in the laws we discuss next, is determined according to your faith.

Read Proverb 3:9-10. What word does God use to describe His desire about our giving?

_____

_____

According to this passage, what will be the result of your simple, joyful obedience?

_____

_____

Read Matthew 6:30. What does God promise in this verse He will do for you when you honor Him with the tithe?

_____

_____

Tradition says that Alexander the Great directed that he be buried with his hands at his side, palms up and open. He wanted all who passed in review to see and be reminded that even though he had conquered the known world and died a powerful, wealthy, influential man, he left the world empty-handed. You and I cannot take it with us.

Read Matthew 6:19-20. What do these verses tell us about real, eternal riches and where we should set our greatest affections?

_____

_____

Read Luke 6:47. What warning does Jesus make about obedience to God?

_____

_____

_____

*If you should put even a little upon a little, and do this often, soon this too would become much.*

—*HESIOD, 700 B.C.*

• THE LAWS OF GIVING AND RECEIVING.

Let's begin this important portion of our study with a key verse.

Read Acts 20:35. What does this verse describe as the greatest blessing we can have?

_____

_____

_____

Not only does God want us to learn trust and obedience, which will result in His ability to bless us beyond measure, He also wants to put the icing on the cake. Try to recall a time when you gave a gift to someone who wasn't expecting it but who really needed it, or when you made an offering to a missionary who was ministering in an area of the world you would never see. It was a joy of great measure.

It's a great joy for God to bless us, and He wants us to have an opportunity to share in that joy. When we give, we pull down the strongholds of selfishness, greed, and avarice and put our lives in perspective.

Read Luke 6:38. Finish the statement below from this verse. _____ *and you shall* _____.

Luke 6:38 gives clear direction. If you use a small cup to bless others, your return will also be measured in a small cup. When you use a larger vessel, the return will be commensurate.

God wants us to give to create the following process and sequence of events:

We give in order to receive, in order to be able to give again, in order to be able to receive again, in order to be able to give again.

This cycle of blessing is unending.

> We don't break God's laws; we only demonstrate them.

The problem is that many people try to hold God hostage. We're seriously in error if we think that the principle of giving and receiving is a "get-rich-quick" scheme. Many of us make the mistake of believing we give in order to receive in order to keep and hoard.

Read II Corinthians 9:7 and Luke 6:45 concerning this problem. In these two verses, what does God say we are if our giving is an attempt at manipulation, done with strings attached?

_____

_____


In Malachi 3:8-10, the Word speaks of criminal behavior on the part of many of God's children regarding the subject of giving. The verse declares,

> Will a man rob God? Yet, ye have robbed me. But ye say, Wherein have we robbed thee? In tithes and offerings. Ye are cursed with a curse: for ye have robbed me, even this whole nation. Bring ye all the tithes into the storehouse, that there may be meat in mine house, and prove me now herewith, saith the LORD of hosts, if I will not open you the windows of heaven, and pour you out a blessing, that there shall not be room enough to receive it.


Iimagine a criminal who is in prison for robbing your family of their possessions. How would your feel if he called you and asked you for money? How can we, as God's children, be so callous and unthinking as to believe God will reward us for this same kind of thievery?


## 3. WORK HARD.

Hard work. It is the glory of mankind. God intended us to learn this important value of character. According to God's plan for the family, we are to earn our bread by the toil and sweat of our brow. Work is satisfying, molds character, and develops gratitude, appreciation, and value.

Read Genesis 3:19. What does it set as the standard for receiving the blessings of God from the earth?

_____


Let's consider some well-known sayings and what they teach us when coupled with God's Word about the important issue of work!


### • IF IT SEEMS TOO GOOD TO BE TRUE, IT PROBABLY IS.

Read Proverb 13:11. Write here how it relates to the above saying.

_____

_____

• **TIME IS MONEY.**

Read Proverb 21:5. How does this verse relate to the above saying?

_____

• **A FOOL AND HIS MONEY ARE SOON PARTED.**

Proverb 20:4 explains what it is that causes a fool and his money to be parted. Write that characteristic here.

_____

_____

• **TALK IS CHEAP.**

Proverbs 24:30-34 expresses clear principles about work and how they relate to the above saying. Write them here.

_____

_____

• **WELL DONE IS BETTER THAN WELL SAID.**

Read Ecclesiastes 5:19. What does this verse teach us about the importance of working to get a job done?

_____

• **INCH BY INCH ANYTHING'S A CINCH.**

Proverbs 21:25 describes the person who wants everything to come easily. What is the key characteristic of the person listed in this verse?

_____

_____

• **PUT YOUR SHOULDER TO THE WHEEL.**

Second Thessalonians 3:10 was written as an admonition to every lazy person that ever lived. What declaration does this verse make?

_____

_____

### 4. MAKE A REALISTIC BUDGET AND KEEP ACCURATE RECORDS.

The culprit in family finance problems is not the big-ticket items. It is the steady drip, drip, drip of spending on little purchases that no one tracks. You hit the ATM machine all weekend and end up broke on Monday with no idea where the money went. The absence of an accurate record of spending keeps couples from making good financial decisions.

Matthew 25:14-30 is a rather lengthy passage, but it describes very clearly what God wants us to do with the resources He gives us. He has a certain plan. Read the entire passage and then write here what you think His plan is and what He will do if we do not follow His guidelines.

_____

_____

_____

_____

One of the most practical passages in the Bible regarding this subject is found in Proverbs 24:3-4. Read to what the verse says from *The Living Bible*:

> *"ANY ENTERPRISE IS **BUILT** BY **WISE PLANNING**, BECOMES STRONG THROUGH **COMMON SENSE**, AND **PROFITS WONDERFULLY** BY **KEEPING ABREAST OF THE FACTS!**"*

We cannot imagine a better plan for a Fortune 500 company than the simple truths in that verse. They certainly are applicable for your family. You must know what is going on with your money or you will be tossed by every wind.

Read Luke 14:28-30. What does this verse suggest to you about a family budget and spending plan?

_____

_____

*Giving should reflect our relationship with God, not our ability to respond to some emotional crisis.*
—*Sylvia Ronsavalle*

Read Proverbs 23:5. This verse describes the very nature of money and what will happen if we do not control our spending. Write down what money will do if you do not budget.

_____

_____

There is another issue in family budgeting. Who will handle the money, pay the bills, and keep these important records? Family finances, of course, are a matter that should be discussed with everyon,e but one person needs to be on top of the day-to-day operation. Everyone needs to be involved in the process, but there needs to be one "general" who is skilled in handling the day-to-day operation of the family budget. In our family Rita is our "financial guru." She is wonderful with the details of money management. In your family it may be the husband or the wife who has these skills, but a manager must be determined. Your family is a small business and must be treated as such.

Read Proverbs 27:23-24. These verses describe the abilities necessary to be the person who handles the money in a family. List those skills here.

_____

_____

_____

Read Proverbs 21:20. Use *The Living Bible* if you can. What does the verse say we are if we violate the principles of good money management?

_____

_____

If you need help in establishing a budget, there are many resources available at bookstores, your bank, and on the Internet that are free of charge and will give you clear assistance in this matter. The key is to get started with a format, which will allocate your resources as well as track your expenses.

**5. GET OUT FROM UNDER THE BONDAGE OF DEBT.**
Your attitude toward money will make a huge difference in the success or failure of your family. A familiar phrase from wedding ceremonies, "'Til death us do part," has tragically become, "'Til *debt* us do part!"

Are you trying to resolve your anxieties by filling the void with the purchase of "stuff"? Do you feel you deserve things since you were poor as a child? Do you want to make sure your children have things so they will impress others? Do you or members of your family make impulse purchases or use that plastic credit card to satisfy the "I-can't-live-without-this-item" urge?

*When poverty comes in the door, love flies out the window.*
—OLD ENGLISH PROVERB

Is your family a family of chronic overspenders? The life of a family of overspenders is often chaotic and marked by a series of crisis events where "creative financing" becomes a month-by-month part of life. How in the world is a family supposed to succeed with this bondage of debt hanging over their heads? Families in this situation think in terms of, "How much will the payment be for this item over a long period of time?" rather than how much the item will actually cost.

Some of you reading this are so far behind you can't even imagine how you will ever get out of debt. Let's consider some basic truths about this problem and clarify an important issue about debt. Debt, which would be labeled "bondage debt," has certain specific characteristics. If you own a home for which you owe

$50,000 and it is valued at $75,000 that is *not* bondage debt. If you have credit card bills which have built up to thousands of dollars, and you no longer even have the disposable items that created the debt, that *is* the bondage debt about which we speak. If the item for which you went into debt does not provide collateral that is worth more than the indebtedness held against it, you have a problem in the making. To get out of debt, follow these principles:

*Can anybody really remember when times were not hard and money was not scarce?*
—RALPH WALDO EMERSON, 1867

### • PAY YOUR BILLS.

Read Psalm 37:21. This verse relates the basic problem of a family in debt. Write that problem here.

_____

_____


What does the verse say is the proper thing to do?

_____

_____


### • GET HELP.

Proverbs 14:11 gives clear direction to a family in debt. They need to take an important step. Write here what the verse says that step is.

_____

_____


In your own words, write a brief statement that expresses why you agree or disagree with the above verse.

_____

_____

_____


Psalm 1:1 describes the two characteristics of a person from whom we should seek help. Write those two characteristics here.

1._____

_____


2._____

_____


### • CHANGE YOUR LIFESTYLE.

There is an important understanding which must be clarified about living in the cycle of debt:

1. We can live **within** our means.

By spending no more than we make each month. This is the correct goal or a successful family.

*or*

2. We can live **above** our means.

By spending more than we make each month. Most families in trouble with debt are at this point.

It is essential that you stop at this moment and make a decision. We cannot begin to tell you what to do in your particular situation. We would need much more personal and detailed information. Our greatest desire would be that you get skilled help from a godly financial counselor immediately. Don't let your pride get in the way! There are many wonderful nonprofit agencies which can help you establish a plan to become debt free. If you choose to ignore the warning signs we have discussed in this chapter, then you can expect your suffering and anxiety to only increase. Remember the admonitions of God's Word about this bondage. Romans 13:8 says, *"Owe no man any thing, but to love one another."* As long as you are in debt, you will be incarcerated in a prison of fear and debilitating powerlessness. Proverb 22:7 reminds us about indebtedness, *"the borrower is servant to the lender."* As long as your family is in debt, you are slaves to the credit card company, bank, or lender. Bondage to anything in the life of a believer is not appropriate. Attack it today!

# TEACH YOUR CHILDREN THESE FIVE IMPORTANT FINANCIAL PRINCIPLES

Read Deuteronomy 4:9 and Deuteronomy 31:13 before you continue with this final section. What do these verses say you, as a parent, are to do for your children regarding the issue of life principles they need to learn? List them here.

_____

_____

_____

### • THE PRINCIPLE OF TRUE WEALTH.

Every child must be taught the definition of true wealth. A proper understanding of God's vision of wealth, as we have discussed earlier in this chapter, will allow your child to make the right decisions regarding finances in their adult life. Children must be taught the importance of saving as part of true wealth.

• THE PRINCIPLE OF GRATITUDE.

How many of us have seen children who have no sense at all of the wonderful power of gratitude? A child who grows up in a family where Mom and Dad do not model and expect gratitude will never learn it on his or her own.

• THE PRINCIPLE OF RESPONSIBILITY.

Parents who love their children teach them to be responsable. A child who is given tasks to complete with a built-in reward for accomplishment will understand that they are in charge of their lives. Children who have not been taught the value of money will not expect to be responsible for it. Unless taught otherwise, children will seek to avoid the pain of assuming responsibility for their own problems and choices. The difficulty we have in accepting responsibility for our behavior lies in the desire to avoid the pain of the consequences of that behavior. Children must be taught otherwise. Children need to learn the joy and responsibility of work and earning their own spending money.

*The source of all discontent is from only two sources, wealth and poverty.*
*—PLATO*

• THE PRINCIPLE OF GENEROSITY.

No child should be allowed to reach adulthood without knowing the importance of generosity. Many times selfishness is at the root of our financial problems. Every child needs to learn the most important lesson any child can learn, to share and not be selfish and egocentric with what they have.

• THE PRINCIPLE OF DELAYED GRATIFICATION.

We want it *now*! One of the greatest signs of maturity of a parent is their ability to personally delay gratification and model that principle to their children. When parents never delay gratification, it seems to the young child the way things should be done. If a child sees his parents always behaving with self-discipline, restraint, dignity, and with a capacity to order their own lives, then the child will learn that this is the way to live. If a child sees his parents are without self-discipline or restraint, then he will believe that this is the way to live.

# CHAPTER 10

# SUCCESSFUL FAMILIES ADMIT WHEN THEY NEED HELP, AND THEY GET IT

*Any kingdom that is divided against itself is being brought to desolation and laid waste, and no city or house divided against itself will last or continue to stand.*
—Matthew 12:25 AMP

*A life unexamined is a life not worth living.*
—PLATO

As a marine during the Vietnam era, I (Richard) learned that it could be a fatal mistake to fall asleep while on guard duty in a combat situation. In a combat situation, you must remain alert.

Christian families are in a combat situation every day. A great tragedy in America is families who are asleep at the post. We are allowing our enemies to overrun our position, and the casualties are overwhelming. The number of divorces and broken homes are at a record high.

Read Mark 14:37. In this verse, Christ asked His disciples a question that could be asked of the modern American family. What was that question? How does it apply to this discussion?

*You are either part of the solution or part of the problem.*
—ELDRIDGE CLEAVER

_____

_____

Can you imagine a military officer who is in danger of losing his entire unit to an enemy attack telling his men, "Don't worry about this battle. Everything will work out fine somehow. I'm not going to ask for reinforcements or air support. I know the enemy has us surrounded, and we're defenseless and out of ammunition, but we'll just ignore them, and they might go away. We certainly wouldn't want to humiliate ourselves before the other companies by asking for help and have them think we have problems we can't take care of by ourselves! Besides, it's none of their concern anyway!" It would never happen. Any commanding officer would be on the radio in a heartbeat calling in air support, asking for reinforcements, and seeking advice from headquarters. He would use every resource or option available to save his men from annihilation.

Many families are just not willing to seek help. The result is that the enemy has overrun our defenses, we are losing the war, and families are facing annihilation because they refuse to "call in the marines!"

Read Isaiah 31:1. Complete the last part of this verse.
*Woe to them that go down to Egypt for help; and stay on horses, and trust in chariots, because they are many; and in horsemen, because they are very strong; but they look not unto the Holy One of Israel, _____*
_____ ____ _____!

Our goal in this chapter is to help families determine when they need to go beyond their own resources and abilities and get outside help. It has been said, "We are our own best counselors." Indeed, there are many problems and issues that can be solved without going outside the family. However, there will be occasions when your family needs outside help. We aren't *always* our own best counselors, and we often cannot see the forest for the trees.

## NINE WARNING SIGNS YOUR FAMILY MAY NOT BE ABLE TO SOLVE ITS OWN PROBLEMS.

Before you continue, read John 8:32. What does this verse say will be the result of being truthful with yourself?

_____

_____

We all know the railroad crossing rule. It applies very well here.

### STOP, LOOK, AND LISTEN.
- STOP thinking things will get better by themselves.
- LOOK at the situation as objectively at you can.
- LISTEN to what you hear your family members say and don't say.

When you tell yourself the truth and stop, look, and listen, you may hear or see that some of the following issues are problems in your family.

## 1. You Go Over the Same Issues Again and Again With No Resolution or Closure.

The constant cycle of repeating arguments about the same problems is a clear sign things aren't working and you need help. The reason issues are repeated is because you aren't presenting information that is being heard, received, or accepted.

## 2. Your Networking Is Not Working.

Every attempt at reasonable conversation fails and ends with shouting, disregard, or someone walking out of the room with no closure or resolution.

## 3. There Is Physical and/or Emotional Abuse.

There is no way you should allow this behavior to continue without getting help and finding safety. Physical, emotional, and verbal abuse should not be tolerated.

## 4. You Pretend to Respect a Family Member Whom You Do Not Really Respect.

This is an indication of a serious problem. One dysfunctional family member rules the rest of the family, usually by fear. When I (Richard) was a child, I never knew how to act until I saw the mood of my alcoholic father. We all acted like we respected him, but it wasn't authentic. We despised him in private, but would not dare say anything openly. We needed help.

## 5. You're Afraid to Say Certain Things in Your Family.

When you don't feel comfortable sharing your feelings and thoughts without being demeaned, criticized, or bullied, something is terribly wrong.

## 6. You Deny, Excuse, or Choose to Ignore the Signs of Problems Such as Drug or Alcohol Abuse.

Substance abuse is an indication of greater problems than simple emotional distress or fatigue. A key issue is when family members excuse the behavior saying, "They can stop anytime; they're not addicted." This is the height of denial, and a key indicator that help is needed.

## 7. You Have a Recurring Wish that You Were Out of Your Family or Had Never Come into It at All.

This kind of negative daydreaming is a result of much deeper problems that need professional help. All of us have occasional wishes we weren't in a family

*I have never failed, not one time in my entire life. I have, however, proven many times what will not work.*

—*Thomas Edison*

or marriage, but when it becomes a daily obsession there should be deeper consideration as to its reason and impact.

### 8. No One Admits a Problem, Yet Everyone Knows It Exists.

Some people think that it is an admission of failure to admit that there's a problem. This avoidance can be fatal to a marriage or family.

### 9. You Ignore or Excuse Signs of Bad Behavior in a Family Member.

Bullying, giving orders, pulling rank, verbal abuse, arrogance, and indifference to the feelings of others are signs of this malady.

Read Luke 14:18. What does this verse say we do to justify our behavior?

_____

_____

## Eight Warning Signs Your Marriage May Be in Trouble

*I am looking for an honest man.*

—*Diogenes*

1. You are constantly irritated with your spouse by the smallest things they do.
2. You have little or no interest in sexual relations with your spouse.
3. There is emotional, verbal, or physical abuse.
4. You prefer being with others more than with your partner.
5. You continually think about divorce and fantasize what life would be like to be married to someone else.
6. You're negative, sarcastic, and critical with your mate, know it's wrong but cannot seem to stop.
7. You argue over the same issues again and again with no closure or resolution.
8. You're addicted to pornography.

## Why Can't We Always Solve Our Own Problems?

The reason is all too simple. Sometimes we lack the skills, resources, abilities, or understanding. If you needed new eyeglasses, would you break the bottoms out of two glass soft drink bottles, get some wire, and make your own because you didn't want to pay a professional to make them? Would you perform a root canal on your own molar with your new power drill? Would you take out your own appendix? Of course not.

When we need glasses, dental work, or medical attention, we go to the experts who are trained in those areas. We don't even give it a second thought. Yet amazing at it may seem, many of us act like we can handle serious family problems by ignoring them or trying to solve them ourselves. Sometimes we act like they'll simply go away on their own. But the problems don't go away, our efforts fail, and the bottom often falls out.

If you cut your finger or get a sunburn, you can go to a local pharmacy and get what you need for self-medication and treatment. There are many things you can do to take care of yourself in certain situations.

There are areas in which you, as parents, need to be skilled enough to solve and resolve issues and problems. But when you see warning signs such as those outlined in this chapter, you need to get help. If you don't seek help for serious, unresolved issues, your family may be doomed to failure.

We would consider anyone on the *Titanic* to have been insane if they had ignored the impending disaster and insisted on rearranging deck chairs instead. Is your family going about your day-to-day schedule (arranging deck chairs) while your home is sinking from the problems? Decide to save yourselves by getting help.

Read Hebrews 5:11-14 which explains why we sometimes cannot help ourselves and need help from others.

• Verse 11 says we need help because we sometimes become what?

_____

_____

• Verses 12-13 say we may be capable teachers in many areas of our lives. It also says we need help and must become students again from time to time. Why?

_____

_____

• Verse 14 concludes by describing the characteristics of a temporary teacher. What is the goal of this teacher? Why have they earned the right to teach us?

_____

_____

*Draw from others the lessons they have learned from whence you may profit yourselves.*

—PUBLIUS TERENTIUS, 159 B.C.

Our desire, and the desire of your heavenly Father is that your family be a-MAZING, not a-MAZE.

As marriage and family counselors, we have often wondered what might have happened with many of the families with whom we were working if they had come to us earlier. Families fall into disarray and eventual failure because they don't recognize, or won't admit to, the warning signs that they're in trouble.

Successful families don't ask, "Why can't we get along?" They ask, "What's keeping us from getting along? Do we need to get help?"

## Four Reasons a Family in Trouble May Not Seek Outside Help.

### • Pride

Scripture admonishes that pride goes before destruction and a haughty spirit before a fall. Many families are failing because of bitter pride and an unwillingness to admit that anything is wrong. We humans are strange creatures who hate to admit failure.

*When pride comes, then comes disgrace, but with humility comes wisdom.* Proverb 11:2 (NIV).

*Pride goeth before destruction, and an haughty spirit before a fall.* Proverb 16:18 (NIV).

*A man's pride shall bring him low.* Proverbs 29:23 (NIV).

### • Ignorance

Many times families simply don't know where to turn. Start by asking your minister. Look in the yellow pages of your telephone directory under the heading "Christian Counselors." If you were dying of a disease you'd find help. This should be equally as critical to you.

*Now, brothers, I know that you acted in ignorance…* Acts 3:17 (NIV).

### • Lack of Cooperation

It's sad, but often true, that one or more members of the family know they need help and want to get it, but they have no cooperation from the rest of the family. The person who needs help the most is usually the hardest sell on the matter. Some people don't want to cooperate because they actually love their suffering. They like trouble and find a sense of value in living on the edge of chaos.

# FOR MY LOVE THEY ARE MY ADVERSARIES: BUT I GIVE MYSELF UNTO PRAYER.
## —PSALM 109:4

Many single moms must take the role as the head of the home. If you are a single mom, then your role is to take the lead in this matter. However, in a two-parent home the great tragedy is the fact that the very person who should be leading the charge to get help, the father, is often the person who drags his feet the most. Men with wives and children who are suffering because of unresolved family issues should be the first to say, "We need to get help."

Winston Churchill said the attack of the German *Luftwaffe* on London and the eventual victory by Great Britain's Royal Air Force was "their finest hour." Dad, your finest hour will come when you set aside your pride and lead your family to the help it needs. We guarantee they will admire you for your efforts in a way that many men never experience. Notice what the following verse says a "good man" will do to protect his family.

*This know, that if the good man of the house had known what hour the thief would come, he would have watched, and not have suffered his house to be broken through.* Luke 12:39

## • MONEY

This can certainly be an understandable problem. How will you afford counseling? Won't it cost hundreds of dollars an hour? Will your insurance cover it? These are all valid questions that should be addressed. However, there are many wonderful sources for Christian counseling that are affordable, non-profit, or pro-bono. You just need to ask. Start with a conversation with your minister.

*A problem completely understood is a problem half solved.*
—*THOREAU*

## FIVE STEPS TO TAKE TO GET HELP.

### 1. ADMIT THERE IS A PROBLEM.

Many counselors believe one of the most important things a family can do in a time of crisis is to reframe the situation by admitting the problem exists. You must look at what is happening to your family from every possible perspective and get help. You can hold a series of family meetings and focus on how you can work together to meet the challenges you face.

Read Psalm 119:28-29. It speaks of the heaviness which many of us have felt when our families struggle. What does the verse say keeps us from moving ahead toward resolution and help?

_____

John Maxwell tells of two college professors from Alabama and Tennessee who placed an ad in fifty newspapers in twenty-five cities which made the same request: "If you live in a strong family, please e-mail us. We know a lot about what makes a family fail. We need to know more about what makes them succeed." Over three thousand people contacted them. The most common response was, "We admit when we have a problem, and we try to do something about it instead of just ignoring it and hoping it will go away."[15]

A minister recently told us that several men in his congregation refused to come to a marriage conference we were leading at a nearby lodge. Their reason? "We don't want to go to that marriage retreat and have people think we have problems in our marriage." The very statement they made indicated their need for the weekend!

What does Proverb 12:15 say a person becomes if they don't believe they need help with their lives or problems?

_____

To admit there might be a problem with which the family needs help presents a moment of crisis to some people. They feel more comfortable sweeping the problem under the rug instead of looking for the potential for growth, renewed health, and healing.

**2. GET A REALISTIC BUT OPTIMISTIC PERSPECTIVE OF THE PROBLEM.**
The Chinese symbol, or pictograph, for the word "crisis," is a composite of two other pictographs: the symbol for "danger" and the symbol for "opportunity." For thousands of years, the Chinese have known that a crisis can be not only a dangerous time, but also a time to look for new opportunities.

DANGER        OPPORTUNITY

CRISIS

Life can be even better and more fulfilling if we can find ways to endure our hardships together. We're not suggesting that you ignore the seriousness of your situation, assume a "head-in-the-sand" attitude, and ignore reality – quite the contrary. This is serious business. We understand that. Families can become so negative that they steal the power that realistic optimism can bring to their efforts. Establish a proper perspective on your family's difficulties by seeing the danger, but also by realizing the wonderful opportunity that lies within the crisis.

Second Corinthians 4:8-9 gives us examples of some optimistic responses to life's challenges. Read the verses and complete the lists below.

We are...

Troubled, but not _____ .

Perplexed, but not _____ .

Persecuted, but not _____ .

Cast down, but not _____ .

*We are not all capable of everything.*

—Virgil Maros, 70 B.C.

Second Corinthians 4:7 tells us why we should have realistic optimism about our problems. Write here what it promises.

_____

_____

If your family can see the situation as not only a serious difficulty but also an opportunity to strengthen your bonds with each other, you can meet the challenge. The key is positive communication with each other. Essentially, if you can find the courage to talk about your problem with each other and with someone else who is skilled in counseling, you can find ways to solve it.

Proverb 14:12 gives a serious warning to those who would continue in negativity and fear about solving their problems all by themselves. What is the result when we try to accomplish solutions on our own?

_____

Families sometimes fall into disarray during times of crisis. But those families who can recover from the initial shock and sense of despair, and band together to find solutions to their difficulties commonly say they feel stronger and more appreciative of each other as family members. "I wouldn't ever want to go through something like that again," people are likely to say, "but I wouldn't take a million dollars for the love we now share. We learned to support and care for each other till the crisis was over."

For a long, long time, human beings have been relying on their creative ability to reframe difficult life situations and see the positive potential in the middle of the problem.

### 3. Ask Every Family Member to Accept Their Responsibility Regarding the Problem.

Each of us must accept responsibility for our own actions. Scripture is very clear about the importance of confessing our faults one to another. Scripture also instructs us to go directly to a person with whom we may have a problem. When there is a problem, every member of the family is affected in one way or another, and every member should be a part of the solution. It is critical to be able to tell one another what needs to be said in order to clear the air.

Exodus 32:24 presents a remarkable study in human nature. According to this verse, what is the characteristic of a person who will not take responsibility for his actions?

_____

_____

In her book *Trial Marriages and the Future of Marriage in America*, Pamela Paul wrote, "One of the scariest things about family is operating in isolation and being afraid to talk about the bad things."[16]

It's incredible how many people we counsel who walk by each other in the hallways of their homes, knowing all along that there are problems, yet not admitting it, opening dialogue, clearing the air, or taking personal responsibility.

Psalm 41:4 and II Samuel 12:13 give two examples of individuals who took responsibility for their actions. Not taking personal responsibility is actually a sin against whom?

_____

_____

T.S. Eliot addressed this issue of how family members become so selfish and egocentric that they lose perspective regarding their personal responsibility.

*Half the harm that is done in this world is due to people who want to feel important. They don't mean to do harm – but they do and the harm they cause does not concern them, or they do not want to see it or be concerned about it, or they justify it because they are absorbed in the endless struggle to think well of themselves.*

## 4. Make Sure You Approach the Problem As a Spiritual, Not an Intellectual Battle

Recognize family problems for what they are, spiritual battles for your family.

Read Ephesians 6:12. What does that verse tell you about the battle you fight each day? Is the conflict with your family members? Write your understanding here.

_____

_____

Second Corinthians 10:4 talks about the powerful strongholds that can become part of our lives. The fortifications that protect the problems the enemy uses to destroy our families can be pulled down by what two forces?

_____

_____

## 5. Find a Skilled, godly Counselor.

You should ask one question when choosing a counselor: "Does this person I'm asking to be a source for me and my family make God and His Word their source?"

Romans 11:34 names the "counselor" used by a "counselor." Who does it name?

_____

Daniel 5:14 lists the characteristics of the counselor you should select to help you and your family. Write those characteristics here.

_____

_____

The individual you select needs to be a spiritually tested, emotionally mature, and stable individual. Ask for references and expect credentials. It is essential that you work with a person who has gained your trust and has an intimate walk with God. Your minister or another professional may be an excellent counselor.

*Defeat may serve as well as victory to shake the soul and let the glory out. When the great oak is straining it sends down roots deeper into the soil. Sorrows come to stretch out spaces in the heart for greater joy.*

—Edwin Markham

Proverb 19:21 says that a good counselor will have wonderful skills but must depend on one factor above all. Write that factor here.

_____

_____

One of the most difficult things for us over the years has been to seek outside help for our own family. We remember how we felt many years ago when we, as a family, went to a Christian counselor to discuss problems we were having which we could not seem to solve ourselves. We felt like failures. But if we hadn't made that decision, and others like it over the years, it's entirely possible that today our family might be in "cardiac arrest," one more statistic of a failed family.

*A lot of people keep their problems and get rid of their partner and only end up having the same issues with the next person.*

*—Diane Plumberg*

## Eight Reasons to Choose an Outside Counselor.

1. They can be objective, seeing things you might not see and offering options you may not want to consider, but need to.

2. They can be emotionally uninvolved and give suggestions and options which are not shaded by anger, resentment, or personal gain or position.

3. They can be skilled listeners and give you the opportunity to express deep-seated feelings, concerns, emotions, and attitudes in a setting of safety and understanding without fear of reprisal or condescension.

4. They can give you biblical insight into God's desire and direction regarding your particular situation, direction that will be the most important advice you can receive. A biblically-based counselor will bring to your sessions the power of the Holy Spirit, the Word of God, and prayer that will have positive impact on the outcome of your situation.

5. They can give you the benefit of their experience from having dealt with others who have been down the same road you're now traveling. Their experience and road map will be invaluable as they guide you into considerations and options that you can use to make decisions as to what you will do.

6. The can give you complete confidentiality in the sessions. A godly counselor will know how important it is for you to be able to speak freely with complete

confidence that you will not hear the information you are sharing repeated anywhere else.

7. They can use tools and skills that are a result of their training and experience, tools that are not going to be available to you and your family if you try to work things out on your own. They have insights and options that will illuminate the problem in ways you might never have considered.

8. They can offer accountability that will be desperately needed. It is not enough to talk about the problem and ramble on with someone about your feelings and concerns. There must be a sense of accountability and progress. A professional counselor will lead you through a process of options, and accountability for action regarding those options, that will create the confidence that you are making positive headway with the problem.

## THINK TWICE BEFORE SEEKING OUTSIDE HELP FROM THE FOLLOWING SOURCES

Read 1 Timothy 5:13: *Besides, they get into the habit of being idle and going about from house to house. And not only do they become idlers, but also gossips and busybodies, saying things they ought not to* (NIV).

• *Social acquaintances* aren't the place to start looking for help. They aren't skilled, but they'll love the gossip. They are usually well-intentioned and may offer moral support, but far too often they take sides and don't have the necessary skill to help.

• *Relatives* are too emotional, have too much vested interest, and aren't going to have the objectivity you need. They should be there for your family in prayer support, but not in taking the lead in attempted resolution and closure.

• *Colleagues at work* are not appropriate counselors. Your employer doesn't want you to bring your dirty laundry from home and make the workplace a counseling room.

• *Non-biblical advisors* should be avoided. Psalm 1:1 makes it very clear. We are not to walk in the counsel of the ungodly. They will give advice based on the reason of man and not on the understanding of God's Word.

*Immature minds usually dismiss anything which reaches beyond their control and understanding.*
—FRANCOIS ROUCHEFOUCALD, 1678

In the ultimate moment of honesty, we show our greatest wisdom. If you seek help when you know the answers are beyond you, you'll find success beyond measure. Your family members will grow in respect for each other and the strength which follows will bind you together with a cord that is not easily broken. However if you continue to muddle along and ignore the signs of problems that plague you, you are doomed to failure.

Don't let Homer's warning in *The Odyssey*, written in 700 B.C. become your family's epitaph.

> *By their own follies and lack of council they perished, the fools. Look now how mortals are blaming the gods, for they say that evils come from them, but in fact, they themselves have woes beyond their share because of their own folly. What a wonderful opportunity to show how much you treasure and value your family by admitting you have a problem that needs help from a skilled, compassionate counselor!*

> *They acknowledge their offence, and seek my face: in their affliction they will seek me early.*
> —Hosea 5:15

When you look back and realize the self-respect and dignity that resulted an strengthened your entire family, the moment you decided to get help will become your "shining moment." Congratulations as you make this critical step. It is what successful families do.

*The greatest weakness of all weaknesses is to fear too much to appear weak.*
—Jacques Bassuet, 1641

# CHAPTER 11

# SUCCESSFUL FAMILIES ESTABLISH POSITIVE MEMORIES AND TRADITIONS

*Hold fast the traditions and instructions which you were taught by us.*
—*2 Thessalonians 2:15* (AMP)

*Webster's Encyclopedia Unabridged Dictionary* defines "traditions" as memories, customs, habits, and information handed down from one generation to another over the years, that become time-honored practices.[17]

Over the years, our family has enjoyed many traditions. We had forgotten how many traditions and positive memories we had until we began writing this chapter. Some were big events that included everyone, while others were small, intimate traditions between two or three family members.

When you find a successful, happy family, you'll find a family with many positive memories and traditions. Positive traditions reaffirm for us that the treasures of the heart are the memories of a life well spent with those you love. These memories become a lasting part of the legacy of the successful family.

We sit on our porch on summer evenings drinking coffee and enjoying the "empty nest" years. We've come full circle now, and have one another again, alone! It is where we started our marriage, and we are delighted to be back. However, as we sit there in the quiet dusk it is rare that we don't begin to reminisce about the past. We love to talk about old memories and traditions we enjoyed with the children and new ones that are emerging with our grandchildren.

In our seminars we often sing a song titled "Hold on to the Years," accompanied by projected images of family. The photographs and lyrics of the song are a poignant reminder of how time certainly does fly, and the memories you have

*Traditions cannot be inherited. They are only gained by effort.*
—*T. S. ELIOT*

*Blood is thicker than water.*
—*ENGLISH PROVERB*

from the traditions you make will become more valuable to you than any bank account balance. Those positive memories are the real stuff of life and the evidence that our family succeeded. We worked at it for years, and the interest payments we're receiving now are wonderful!

Make memories!!

Read Psalm 90:12 and Proverb 17:6. What do these verses suggest are the wisest things we can do with our time? What is true joy?

_____

_____

Making and keeping positive traditions is the serious business of the family. Proverb 17:22 describes a family in which everything is always serious and heavy. What prescription does this verse give for parents to fill and administer in their family?

_____

_____

## TRADITIONS ACHIEVE THREE RESULTS IN SUCCESSFUL FAMILIES.

### 1. TRADITIONS BRING A FAMILY TOGETHER, CAUSING THE MEMBERS TO KNOW ONE ANOTHER BETTER.

# TRADITIONS ARE IMPORTANT TO EVERYONE, AND ARE DIFFERENT FOR EVERYONE.

When you look at a family from the outside what you're seeing is a result of their traditions kept on the inside.

We have a "Wall of Fame" in our house (which eventually spilled over to the walls of the garage), which displays every plaque, team photo, award, and trophy our children ever won. It means nothing to anyone else, but it's priceless to us. It is a reminder of many events that brought us together as a family.

Our daughter, Trinity, and her brother David have a secret code, "BBLS," whose meaning is known only to them. We would all give anything to know what it means, but have decided we never will. It's their private tradition.

We always placed paper victory signs on the garage door the morning after the boys' football games.

We built a treehouse with sheer determination and zero skill.

Your memories and traditions may be similar to ours or quite different, but their value should be centered on being together as a family.

ESTABLISHING TRADITIONS BEGINS WITH AND IS THE RESPONSIBILITY OF THE PARENTS. A couple must begin establishing traditions long before the first child arrives. This will set the stage for a lifelong pursuit of great traditions that create wonderful bonding memories. Parents must establish the goal of "memory making" when their marriage is new and their children are tiny.

Some traditions are created. Some evolve. Some just happen.

We created a favorite family tradition of putting up the Christmas tree each Thanksgiving afternoon, but the tradition of our annual family football game that same day simply happened while we were together as a family. Both traditions have accompanying positive memories and are almost twenty years old, but they have completely different roots. Some memories you make. Some just happen. But they are all created when you're simply being together as a family.

You and your spouse must decide together to be in charge of making positive memories for your family. Determine on an event-by-event basis whether or not a particular activity will create a positive memory. Work to keep these kinds of tradition-making events in your family's schedule.

The effectiveness of family traditions is directly related to the degree that parents actively cultivate them. It's up to parents, therefore, to make a conscious effort to invest their time, energy, and personal presence in order to celebrate traditions in ways that create a sense of belonging for each family member. You must build a binding link among generations by developing memories that can be enriching to children and parents alike.

*Every tradition grows more venerable as the years pass...until they finally inspire awe.*

*—NIETZSCHE*

**Traditions Often Begin as Magical, Miraculous Moments.**

Many events which become lasting traditions were unexpected and unplanned. We call them "magical, miraculous moments."

Magical, miraculous moments come to families who talk with one another, play together, and have decided to love one another in complete acceptance. Traditions will establish themselves if you simply allow yourself to be a part of your family. When you least it expect it, a tradition will emerge with a great memory on its heels.

Our son David's impromptu gift of a stuffed bear for our daughter-in-law Pam one Christmas has created a memory for both of them that has become a significant tradition in their marriage. Now every Christmas Pam receives a bear, a token of their commitment to one another.

**2. Traditions Create Positive Memories Which Can Provide Encouragement and Stability.**

*The joy of life is its variety of traditions. The tenderest love is rekindled by their memories.*

—*Samuel Johnson, 1753*

# Traditions Are Memories of Memories

Great moments that evolve into empowering family traditions don't happen on command. They occur when you least expect it.

When you sit alone with your thoughts, what do you usually think of? You remember wonderful traditions, memories, and the magic moments, we are drawn to a secure base called "family." God wants families to be bound together by this wonderful adhesive of positive experience and tradition. These memories can be the "glue" in difficult times that holds a family together.

The memories which accompany our traditions can have a powerful impact. As recorded in Psalm 137:1, while the children of Israel were in captivity what was their response regarding their memories?

_____

_____

No one can understand your memory, embrace it, or appreciate it as much as you. That's what makes it so special for a successful family. It binds you with your family members in a special way that no one else can share, join, or understand. It is an exclusive club.

### 3. TRADITIONS ARE CHERISHED AND PASSED ALONG TO FUTURE GENERATIONS.

Traditions build relationships, memories, and foundations. Positive family traditions can be empowering and immensely rewarding. The desire to establish traditions speaks volumes about your attitude toward your family. We don't want to establish traditions with people for whom we have no love, respect, or admiration.

Deuteronomy 32:7 gives very clear instructions regarding how we are to pass traditions and positive memories from generation to generation. How does this verse say this important work is to be accomplished?

_____

The interaction and bonding our traditions create play a great part in the development of a caring and stable family environment that can be passed on to future generations.

Read Proverb 14:26. What kind of environment does this verse say a child will experience when parents pass on God's love from one generation to the next?

_____

_____

In *The Fiddler On The Roof*, at his daughter's wedding, Tevye sings a song which echoes traditions and memories that move from one generation to another:

> *Is this the little girl I carried? Is this the little boy at play? I don't remember growing older, when did they? Sunrise, sunset, sunrise, sunset, quickly fly the years. One season following another, laden with happiness and tears.*[18]
> —SUNRISE, SUNSET

His words are all about tradition and the sweet memories they bring. Another memorable song from the musical is titled "Tradition!" A portion of its lyrics include the following words.

> *Tradition? The papa, tradition…the mama, tradition…the son and the daughter, tradition…a family? Tradition, Tradition, Tradition!*

Cherished traditions and memories give our families a sense of who they are, from whence they came, and where they are going. Positive traditions give us a sense of stability and belonging, which we all desperately need. Traditions make

*Americans feel anchored in their memories.*
—NORMAN MAILER

us feel safer and more stable during turbulent times. They become our identifiers that there is one place, our family, where we can find stability in the world. They are worth all the work you might have to do to create them.

## FAMILIES WITH FEW POSITIVE TRADITIONS OR MEMORIES EXHIBIT THREE CHARACTERISTICS:

1. They have nothing in common since they do nothing together.
2. They are fearful of the closeness which leads to intimacy.
3. They have little trust for one another and basically live separate lives.

These three characteristics of unsuccessful families are a result of the absence of positive traditions. These families have a terrible instability when it comes to their family history. All the memories seem to be ones everyone wants to forget. "Dysfunctional families have few meaningful traditions, and some very dysfunctional traditions," says Franklin Olson, a family counselor in Houston, Texas. "Healthy families, on the other hand, have very meaningful traditions."[17]

Unhealthy families only remember days clouded with storms and torrential downpours of problems and anguish. They have nothing to celebrate.

Proverb 10:7 tells us about the memories of the just and of the wicked. What does the verse say shall be the legacy (or memories) of the just?

_____

_____

_____

What will be the legacy (memories) of the family with no positive memories or traditions?

_____

_____

_____

Bad memories are not part of God's plan. The family is to be a place of celebration, a happy place, a safe haven. Families with no positive traditions will have great difficulty succeeding. The traditions and memories of these families do not lead to a positive legacy of cohesive love for one another, but to a negative legacy which is passed from one generation to the next.

You establish positive memories by placing yourself in circumstances that allow magical moments to happen. You'll never know the joy of swimming in the ocean if you never go to the beach. Creating important memories for your family only happens if you make a conscious decision to do things together.

In today's hectic world, families are frequently uprooted. This can make it difficult for children to acquire a sense of continuity and security. Family traditions are so very important for children to develop feelings of safety and dependability. The way families celebrate holidays or even interact at mealtime will play a vital role in establishing and perpetuating a healthy lifestyle of positive traditions and memories for your family.

Joel 1:3 gives instructions regarding traditions and family history. According to this verse, what is the responsibility of each parent?

_____

_____

**SEVEN IDEAS FOR BUILDING POSITIVE MEMORIES AND TRADITIONS.**
The following are a few ideas that worked well for our family. You might want to try these, or you can come up with your own. Be creative – your children will love you for it, and your family will grow because of it!

1. FAMILY NIGHT.
Choose one night a week in which the family determines to be together. It might include dinner at home or at a favorite restaurant. Allow your children to help make the decision as to what you will do. Turn off the television. Talk, laugh, and play together. Wrestle on the floor and do things that require talking to one another. Sitting in a movie theater staring at a screen is not a great family night, unless you make time to interact before and after the show. Family night must be a commitment that is honored. Allow nothing to come before it.

2. DATE NIGHT.
One of the most important traditions is any family is an established date night for Mom and Dad. It creates a positive picture for the children as they see their parents choose one night a week to be alone together and to focus on their love for each other. Early in our marriage we could only afford cheap cheeseburgers in the park or a quiet drive, but the goal was intimacy, not extravagance.

*Let us contemplate the traditions of our forefathers and resolve to maintain them as we have learned from the former, to benefit those who come the latter.*
—SAMUEL ADAMS, 1771

### 3. BIRTHDAYS.

Everyone in the family should feel special on their birthday. Always remember that no one likes to have their birthday forgotten! It doesn't cost much money to celebrate that day with great importance and fanfare. The birthday person might get breakfast in bed to begin their day. Be creative. It is a special day loaded with opportunities for family traditions and memories.

### 4. MEALTIME.

What's the most powerful place in your home? The dining room able!!! Turn off the television and eat together. Rita rarely allowed a day to go by that we did not sit down as a family and eat around the dinner table. The conversation was usually electric, hilarious, and invigorating. Some of our greatest memories are from those dinner-table conversations.

### 5. YOUR FAITH.

Spiritual traditions play an important part in the family. Saying grace before meals is one way for a family to connect with each other every day. Daily Scripture reading and prayer times will create wonderful memories. Worshiping together can enhance communication among family members. In addition to attending church together, make it a point for your family to attend special events in your church such as candlelight services, special performances, or special Christmas or Easter services each year.

### 6. FAMILY VACATIONS.

Circle the date on the calendar, buy the film, and don't let anything get in the way! Loads of great memories are created from time spent with your family on vacation. One of our most memorable times was our camping trip to the mountains when it rained like Noah still needed to build the ark! We talk to this day about how much fun we had despite the constant downpour.

The goal of a good, tradition-building vacation is not how much money you spend or how many miles you log but how much fun you have! Some of the most enjoyable things we ever did were road trips. Those one-day excursions at the drop of a hat were more fun than a day spent at any amusement park. Vacation together and make positive memories and traditions.

### 7. HOLIDAYS.

Holidays are perfect for establishing traditions and making memories. They're the "mother lode" of opportunities.

*A man lives not only his personal life, but the story of the life of his family.*

—THOMAS MANN, 1924

A couple attending one of our seminars in Clovis, New Mexico shared a "magical moment" that became one of their family traditions. It started when they were just, being a family. When their children were small, they each tried to hang their Christmas stockings on the fireplace mantle; but each attempt failed because the slippery stone of the fireplace, coupled with the weight of the stockings caused them to fall time after time. After several days of total frustration, the children decided to replace the stockings with cowboy boots! The Christmas cowboy boots sat proudly in front of the fireplace and have replaced traditional stockings every Christmas since then. It was a magical moment that became a wonderful tradition.

Our annual Thanksgiving afternoon football game, "The Tate Family Holiday Bowl" as we call it, has evolved into an event that is now in its eighteenth consecutive year! The "Holiday Bowl" tradition comes complete with specially made shirts for each family member with their name imprinted on the back, and that year's Tate Family Holiday Bowl logo on the front. Photographs grace our dens and living rooms of past contests that have occurred from Abilene, Texas to San Diego, California.

We have never missed putting up the Christmas tree on Thanksgiving afternoon. Traditions, traditions, traditions – they are the gold mines in which the positive memories of successful families are nourished.

Families have such a short window of opportunity to make these memories and establish traditions.

How does James 4:14 describe life's brevity?

_____

_____

Everyone needs to belong somewhere. Even hardened gang members claim the reason they join a gang is because they need to belong. Perhaps the greatest benefit of traditions for your family is to provide members with a way to connect and identify with their family, to be a part of something greater than themselves. Traditions and the accompanying positive memories provide them with hope for tomorrow's memories.

*All love in a family is born with the pleasure of looking at each other, it is fed by the necessity of being with each other, and it is concluded with the impossibility then of being separated from each other.*

—*JOSE MARTI, 1881*

Make time to sit down with your family and discuss your traditions as well as any new traditions you would like to see established. List them below.

_____

_____

_____

_____

_____

_____

_____

_____

_____

_____

_____

_____

_____

_____

_____

_____

_____

# BIBLIOGRAPHY

[1]Michael McManus, *The Marriage Savers,* (Zondervan Publishing, 1995).

[2]Gingrich, Arndt, Danker, Bauer, *Greek-English Lexicon of the New Testament and Other Early Christian Literature,* (Zondervan Publishing House, 1988).

[3]Ibid.

[4]Sir Roy Calne, *The Science Citation Index Report,* (Cambridge University Press, 1997).

[5]George Barna, *Ministering to the Family,* (Barna Research Group, 1989).

[6]Alfred Russel Wallace, *Letters and Reminiscences-Volume One,* (New Amsterdam Book Company, 1916).

[7]John Maxwell, *Think on These Things,* (Thomas Neslson, 1998)).

[8]Eliot R. Smith, *Personality and Social Psychology Review,* (Journal Press, 2001).

[9]Howard J. Faulkner and Virginia Pruitt, *The Selected Correspondence of Karl Menninger,* (University of Missouri Press, 1997).

[10]John Gottman, *Why Marriages Succeed or Fail,* (Fireside Press, 1995).

[11]Aldous Huxley, *Brave New World,* (Harper & Row Publishers, Inc., 1932).

[12]C. S. Lewis, *The Screwtape Letters,* (Harper Collins Publishing,1968).

[13]James Patterson and Peter Kim, *The Day America Told the Truth,* Prentice Hall Press, 1991).

[14]Elisabeth Elliot, *Through Gates of Splendor,* (Tyndale House Publishers, 1955, 1986).

[15]John Maxwell, Ibid.

[16]Pamela Paul, *The Starter Marriage and the Future of Matrimony,* (Villard Books, 2002).

[17]*Webster's Encyclopedic Unabridged Dictionary,* (Random House Publishers, 1996).

[18]Jerry Bock and Sheldon Harnick, "Sunrise Sunset," *Fiddler on the Roof,* (BMG Music, 1964).

# COVENANT MARRIAGE
# AFFIDAVIT AND ATTESTATION FOR COUPLES WHO ARE UNMARRIED

BEFORE ME, the undersigned Notary Public, personally came and appeared:

_____ and _____ who being duly

(NAME OF BRIDE)                 (NAME OF GROOM)

deposed and saying that they received premarital counseling from

_____, _____

(NAME OF COUNSELOR)                  (TITLE OF COUNSELOR)

which counseling included a discussion of the seriousness of covenant marriage, a communication of the fact that a covenant marriage is a commitment for life, a discussion of the obligation to seek marital counseling in time of marital difficulties, and a discussion of the grounds for legally terminating a covenant marriage by divorce.

_____       _____

(SIGNATURE OF BRIDE)                 (SIGNATURE OF GROOM)

ALSO BEFORE ME, the undersigned Notary Public, personally came and appeared:

_____ who being duly sworn, deposed and said that _____ counseled the above man and woman as to the purpose of marriage and the grounds of termination thereof.

_____

(SIGNATURE OF COUNSELOR)

SWORN TO AND SUBSCRIBED BEFORE ME THIS _____ DAY OF _____, 20_____.

_____

(SEAL AND SIGNATURE OF NOTARY PUBLIC)

# COVENANT MARRIAGE
## AFFIDAVIT AND ATTESTATION FOR COUPLES WHO ARE MARRIED

BEFORE ME, the undersigned Notary Public, personally came and appeared:

_____ and _____ who being duly
(NAME OF WIFE)                          (NAME OF HUSBAND)

sworn by me, Notary, deposed and stated that:

Affiants acknowledge that they have discussed their intent to designate
their marriage as a Covenant Marriage with a priest, minister, rabbi, clerk of
the Religious Society of Friends, clergyman of any religious sect,
or a marriage counselor, which included:

A discussion of the obligation to seek marital counseling
in time of marital difficulties, and

A discussion of the exclusive grounds for legally terminating a
Covenant Marriage by divorce.

_____
(SIGNATURE OF WIFE)

_____
(SIGNATURE OF HUSBAND)

SWORN TO AND SUBSCRIBED BEFORE ME THIS _____ DAY OF _____, 20_____.

_____
(SEAL AND SIGNATURE OF NOTARY PUBLIC)

_____
WITNESS:                                    COUNSELOR

# NOTES

# Real Problems... Real People... Real Life... Real Answers...

## THE INDISPUTABLE POWER OF BIBLE STUDIES

**Through the Bible in One Year**
Alan B. Stringfellow • ISBN 1-56322-014-8

**God's Great & Precious Promises**
Connie Witter • ISBN 1-56322-063-6

**Preparing for Marriage God's Way**
Wayne Mack • ISBN 1-56322-019-9

**Becoming the Noble Woman**
Anita Young • ISBN 1-56322-020-2

**Women in the Bible — Examples To Live By**
Sylvia Charles • ISBN 1-56322-021-0

**Pathways to Spiritual Understanding**
Richard Powers • ISBN 1-56322-023-7

**Christian Discipleship**
Steven Collins • ISBN 1-56322-022-9

**Couples in the Bible — Examples To Live By**
Sylvia Charles • ISBN 1-56322-062-8

**Men in the Bible — Examples To Live By**
Don Charles • ISBN 1-56322-067-9

**In His Hand**
Patti Becklund • ISBN 1-56322-068-7

**In Everything You Do**
Sheri Stout • ISBN 1-56322-069-5

**7 Steps to Bible Skills**
Dorothy Hellstern • ISBN 1-56322-029-6

**Great Characters of the Bible**
Alan B. Stringfellow • ISBN 1-56322-046-6

**Great Truths of the Bible**
Alan B. Stringfellow • ISBN 1-56322-047-4

**The Trust**
Steve Roll • ISBN 1-56322-075-X

**Because of Jesus**
Connie Witter • ISBN 1-56322-077-6

**The Quest**
Dorothy Hellstern • ISBN 1-56322-078-4

**God's Solutions to Life's Problems**
Dr. Wayne Mack & Nathan Mack • ISBN 1-56322-079-2

**A Hard Choice**
Dr. Jesús Cruz Correa & Dr. Doris Colón Santiago
ISBN 1-56322-080-6

**11 Reasons Families Succeed**
Dr. Richard & Rita Tate • ISBN 1-56322-081-4

**Rare & Beautiful Treasures**
Nolene Niles • ISBN 1-56322-071-7

**Love's Got Everything To Do With It**
Rosemarie Karlebach • ISBN 1-56322-070-9

# Problemas reales... Gente real... Vida real... Respuestas reales...

## EL INDISCUTIBLE IMPACTO DE LOS ESTUDIOS BÍBLICOS

**A través de la biblia en un año**
Alan B. Stringfellow • ISBN 1-56322-061-X

**Preparando el matrimonio en el camino de Dios**
Wayne Mack • ISBN 1-56322-066-0

**Mujeres en la Biblia**
Sylvia Charles • ISBN 1-56322-072-5

**Parejas en la Biblia**
Sylvia Charles • ISBN 1-56322-073-3

**Decisión Difícil**
Dr. Jesús Cruz Correa y Dra. Doris Colón Santiago
ISBN 1-56322-074-1